Wishing you
much success
and I look forward
oto to reading
your first
book —
DAVID

# TELLING OUR STORIES

## A HISTORY OF DIVERSITY AT THE UNIVERSITY OF WISCONSIN-MILWAUKEE, 1956–2022

CHIA YOUYEE VANG AND DAVID J. PATE JR., EDITORS

UNIVERSITY of WISCONSIN
UWMILWAUKEE

*Telling Our Stories: A History of Diversity at the University of Wisconsin-Milwaukee, 1956–2022*

Chia Youyee Vang and David J. Pate Jr., Editors

ISBN: 978-0-578-28743-0

Managing editor: Priscilla Pardini
Fact-checker: Elizabeth Hoover
Proofreader: Jenny Gavacs
Design and production: Kou Vang

University of Wisconsin-Milwaukee
P.O. Box 413
Milwaukee, WI 53201
https://uwm.edu/

This book is dedicated to all who came before us.

CONTEN

# DREAMER

*Telling Our Stories: A History of Diversity at the University of Wisconsin-Milwaukee, 1956–2022* is a book about the power of collective voice and resilience, perseverance against the odds, and in particular, diverse groups of people and how they contributed to what the University of Wisconsin-Milwaukee (UWM) is today—a regional powerhouse that is the most diverse campus in the University of Wisconsin System, one of the nation's top-tier research universities as recognized by the Carnegie Classification of Institutions of Higher Education, and one of the nation's top universities for community engagement, according to the Carnegie Foundation for the Advancement of Teaching.

Aside from countless articles, websites, and books or chapters on specific schools and colleges at UWM, to my knowledge, there have been five books written about UWM's history: *A Brief History of the University of Wisconsin-Milwaukee* (Richard, 1960), *UWM Buildings: Some Pertinent Facts* (Woods, 1960), *The University of Wisconsin-Milwaukee: An Urban University* (Klotsche, 1972), *The History of the University of Wisconsin-Milwaukee: A Historical Profile, 1885–1992* (Cassell, Klotsche, and Olson, 1992), and *University of Wisconsin-Milwaukee, The First Sixty Years, 1956–2016* (Schroeder, 2018). Each admirably covers a specific period of history written from their authors' points of view. However, what none of these books examine is the important role that different dimensions of diversity and inclusion have played in our campus's history. Equally important, none speak with the authenticity of diverse voices that can personally attest to the origins, contributions, and lasting impact such diversity has had on UWM's students, faculty, and staff, as well as on the greater Milwaukee community and even the world.

*Telling Our Stories*, commissioned to showcase these important developments in our

*Mark A. Mone, PhD*

history, fills that void in nine chapters written from the viewpoints of diverse colleagues who continue to define and shape the UWM story.

The result is a recitation of contributions that, together, paint a rich mosaic of the cultural enrichment that UWM alone provides to the region, the state of Wisconsin, and beyond. We take pride today in being not only the most diverse campus on many dimensions—race, sexual orientation, military friendly, first generation, nontraditional, religion, age—but also the only campus that is both a Carnegie Research I university and one with an explicit access mission: we exist to serve all students, and, in particular, those who are historically underrepresented, low income, or first generation—students who all too often have few post-secondary options. These chapters show that as UWM evolved to meet the highest of research standings and to support a diverse student body, it became a home for all, one that uniquely celebrates everything a university should uphold—an intermixing of different backgrounds, experiences, viewpoints, needs, and aspirations.

This journey has not always been easy or smooth. Indeed, in several chapters, readers will learn of ongoing tension among budgets, social forces, competing alternatives, and leadership transitions. And yet a constant thread in this work has been the collective voice of students, faculty, and staff working alongside the community. This speaks to the value of shared governance and a campus that both serves and is responsive to its various communities' needs. It is this latter quality, as documented throughout *Telling Our Stories*, that underscores why we have been recognized as a Carnegie Community Engaged university.

The authors have masterfully captured examples of the progress made across major pillars of diversity—pointing out who the key players were and how they addressed and often overcame hardships to forge one of the leading urban research universities in the nation. The result is many firsts or "only in Wisconsin" achievements: the first campus in the UW System with Black and Latino chancellors and Indigenous and Black tenured faculty, one of the first two universities nationally with a program in African and African Diaspora Studies, a top-level "military friendly" campus that enrolls the largest population of student veterans in the state, and the UW System's first campus to institute Lesbian, Gay, Bisexual, and Transgender (LGBT) Studies and one that consistently ranks among the top LGBTQ+ friendly in the nation. Readers will learn how UWM led the state, and in many ways the nation, in programs serving those with disabilities, and discover that Black graduates of our economics program became editors of the only two journals in the country that examine race and economics. These are just a few of the many remarkable contributions found in this collection.

It may be tempting to believe that the impressive accomplishments attributable to diverse faculty, staff, and administrators were the result of deliberate, intentional efforts. Indeed, that was the case in some areas, as in the strategic efforts to internationalize UWM that began with Chancellor J. Martin Klotsche's foresightful planning, international sabbatical trips, and resulting faculty and student exchange programs. Similarly, UWM's origins included a deliberately strong military veteran focus, with 25 percent of our student body made up of veterans during the 1956–1957 academic year, the year we became UWM. However, in many cases, there was clearly a push and pull, with many student, faculty, and community members' voices being powerful change agents. With the history shared here, readers will appreciate more fully the development of our Women's Resource Center, Roberto Hernández Center, American Indian Studies program, and several other such entities. The essence of these challenges is captured well in Gwynne Kennedy and Merry Wiesner-Hanks's chapter on women at UWM, in which they note, "Pressure for change at academic institutions across the country on women's issues came not only from the federal government, but also from the students, faculty, and staff."

All in all, *Telling Our Stories* informs and inspires. One cannot read the book without being impressed by the leadership that came from all levels to shape the UWM of today. It is a tremendous compilation and a testament to the collective power of many who preceded us to create experiences described in several areas as transformational—for students, faculty, staff, and those in Wisconsin and beyond.

One of the conclusions that I draw from these chapters is that as steadfast and accomplished as we have become in our diversity and inclusion efforts, there is much work in front of us. This book is, accordingly, a marker in two respects: First, it is a how-to manual for accomplishing significant change, demonstrating that although change in academe does not often come easily or quickly, it does occur and can have substantial impact at the scale of a university. Second, it draws a line at a point from which we cannot revert; indeed, I see this book as a challenge to view these accomplishments and where we are today as starting points for a future to which we must commit continued and increased efforts to become even more a university that *welcomes all and ensures their success* in education, research, careers, and community engagement and enrichment.

We owe deep gratitude to several individuals who made this book a reality. First, Vice-Chancellor Emerita Joan M. Prince gets my thanks for bringing the kernel of this book's premise to me; as Joan knows, we both believed the time was right—if not overdue—for this important platform to showcase the valued contributions and accomplishments of diverse groups on our campus. There would be no book if not for the amazing talents and choreography of UWM Professor Chia Youyee Vang (History) and Associate Professor David J. Pate Jr. (Social Work) who coedited the work here. They were effective cheerleaders and taskmasters who moved this book along in a timely, productive way. Fittingly, Professor Vang, during this book's gestation, became Vice-Chancellor of Diversity, Equity, and Inclusion, and will help lead our campus's progress on all dimensions of diversity. I finally add my thanks to Chief of Staff Sue Weslow for her organization, budgeting, and coordination of activities that smoothed the path for publication.

Mark A. Mone, PhD
Chancellor
University of Wisconsin-Milwaukee
June 2022

# PREFACE

Chia Youyee Vang, PhD

It has been a privilege, as well as a great responsibility, for us to have overseen the publication of *Telling Our Stories: A History of Diversity at the University of Wisconsin-Milwaukee, 1956–2022*. As the first of the various histories written about the University of Wisconsin-Milwaukee (UWM) to reflect the voices and lived experiences of underrepresented populations, women, and other marginalized groups, its publication is long overdue.

Over the last sixty-six years, UWM has evolved from a comprehensive university enrolling very few Black, Latino, Asian, or Indigenous students to one of the country's top-tier research universities offering academic programs in all those areas—as well as in Women's & Gender Studies—and providing a range of services and opportunities for students with disabilities, student veterans and other military-related personnel, and international students. Yet nowhere, until now, have the stories about these accomplishments been documented so intentionally. Nowhere, until now, have the voices of those responsible been heard so clearly. Showcasing this work, and the individuals behind this work, has been a pleasure.

We acknowledge as well that the contributions of the students, staff, and faculty at UWM's two regional campuses (UWM at Waukesha and UWM at Washington County) to our diversity and equity work has been essential and have contributed to the richness of the region. *Telling Our Stories*, however, focuses on UWM's main campus in Milwaukee.

By 2020, in the wake of the global Black Lives Matter movement, many institutions were reexamining the impact of race on their organizations. UWM was no exception, with Chancellor Mark A. Mone and then-Vice-

David J. Pate Jr., PhD

Chancellor of Global Inclusion & Engagement Joan M. Prince expressing interest in better understanding and more fully documenting the ways that diverse groups have contributed to UWM. At the time, Chia Youyee Vang served as Associate Vice-Chancellor of Global Inclusion & Engagement and David J. Pate Jr. as coleader of a faculty action team examining issues related to recruitment and retention of faculty. A series of conversations led to the idea for this book, with all of us welcoming the opportunity to learn about the diverse groups on our campus.

Although we had each been at UWM for a decade and a half, we knew we had much to learn; more importantly, we did not believe we could accurately tell UWM's diverse history by ourselves. After some thoughtful debate, we decided on the book's title, *Telling Our Stories: A History of Diversity at the University of Wisconsin-Milwaukee, 1956–2022*, and subsequently invited others with content expertise to contribute.

As we set out to write this book, our campus joined the nation and the rest of the world in trying to figure out how to respond to both the global Covid-19 pandemic and mounting civil unrest. We watched with disappointment and sadness as Americans wrestled with issues of race and racism in apparent futility. As a result, the purpose of this book—to highlight the many positive contributions of colleagues whose significant contributions to UWM's mission have long gone undocumented—took on even more significance.

As we learn more about UWM's history, we acknowledge that we stand on the shoulders of faculty standouts such as Ernest Spaights and staff members such as Leonard White who fought for greater access for underrepresented students. We also recognize the countless students, staff, and faculty throughout the university's history who fought for gender and racial equity. And we are grateful as well for the work of the former UW System Institute on Race and Ethnicity, housed on our campus from 1987 to 2010, whose leaders (Winston Van Horne, Adrian Chan, Tom Tonnesen, and Joyce Kirk) made significant contributions to diversity initiatives across all UW campuses.

We thank Chancellor Mone and Vice-Chancellor Emerita Prince for giving us this opportunity to help document the stories of so many diverse campus community members—both past and present. Sue Weslow, chief of staff in the Office of the Chancellor, facilitated the process to secure the resources needed and Howie Magner and Michelle Johnson in University Relations & Communications assisted us in putting together an excellent editorial and production team. Priscilla Pardini expertly managed the project with her team, and we cannot imagine the final product without her patience and dedication.

Contributors relied on a variety of source material: documents retrieved from the Archives Department of the UWM Libraries; information provided by the university's colleges, schools, programs, and other units; and interviews and correspondence with and personal reflections from individuals with first-hand knowledge of UWM's diversity journey.

To that end, we benefitted from the support provided by Associate Vice-Provost and Director of UWM Libraries Michael Doylen and the UWM Archives staff, Jonathan Hanes in the Office of Assessment & Institutional Research, and Carla Sagert in the Department of Human Resources. We would also like to express our gratitude to staff and alumni for their willingness to work with us and our contributors for filling in the gaps in previous history books and for providing photographs and other images to illustrate this new version of that story.

Finally, we thank our contributors for telling these stories, and are especially grateful to Distinguished Professor Emerita of History Merry Wiesner-Hanks, Professor Emeritus of Educational Psychology Adrian Chan, and Professor Emeritus of Sociology William Vélez for taking part in this project.

This collection makes visible the actions and experiences of individuals and groups that continue to shape who we are today. It demonstrates both how far we have come and how much more our campus will need to do to recognize and include the voices and perspectives of all who are a part of the UWM family.

Chia Youyee Vang, PhD
Vice-Chancellor and Professor of History
University of Wisconsin-Milwaukee

David J. Pate Jr., PhD
Chair and Associate Professor of Social Work
University of Wisconsin-Milwaukee
June 2022

**TELLING OUR STORIES:** A HISTORY OF DIVERSITY AT THE UNIVERSITY OF WISCONSIN-MILWAUKEE, **1956–2022**

## CHAPTER 1

# A Confluence of Contributions: The Indigenous Experience at UWM

MICHAEL WILSON AND
MARGARET NOODIN

*Professor of English Kimberly M. Blaeser reading a poem at the University of Wisconsin-Milwaukee (UWM) Electa Quinney Institute for American Indian Education's fire circle, November 2021. Photo by Chia Youyee Vang.*

An Indigenous presence along the western shores of Lake Michigan extends back thousands of years. The land where the University of Wisconsin-Milwaukee (UWM) sits was used for millennia as a gathering place by many beings after the Laurentide Ice Sheet melted and created a fertile region defined by the confluence of Milwaukee's three rivers. In 2015, UWM students, staff, and faculty began using the following statement to tell a part of the story of this place: "We acknowledge in Milwaukee that we are on traditional Potawatomi, Ho-Chunk and Menominee homeland along the southwest shores of Michigami, North America's largest system of freshwater lakes, where the Milwaukee, Menominee and Kinnickinnic rivers meet and the people of Wisconsin's sovereign Anishinaabe, Ho-Chunk, Menominee, Oneida and Mohican nations remain present."

This statement affirms the distant past of Mississippian, Copper Culture, and Red Ochre Culture ancestors of the Ho-Chunk and Menominee people whose creation stories place them in this region as original people, not immigrants. Many migrations took place and over time they were joined by other Indigenous groups including the Anishinaabe, a large diaspora including the Potawatomi, Ojibwe, and Odawa. The region was preserved, protected, and cultivated by these Indigenous groups until the establishment of New France in 1534, when their stewardship of the region was challenged. Much later, the removal and relocation of eastern nation citizens led to the establishment of the Oneida and Mohican nations west of Lake Michigan, and they began to share in the work of stewarding the territory and bringing the knowledge of their own languages and cultures to the area.

It is important to remember the true history of the land that is now the main Kenwood campus at UWM. Milwaukee was considered uncolonized territory and known as "Indian Reserve" by New France until 1763 when French colonization in the region ended with the ceding of colonial rights to Great Britain and Spain. In 1763, Milwaukee became part of a region Great Britain referred to as the Province of Quebec. Although the United States declared its independence in 1776 and formally ended its Revolutionary War in 1783 with the Treaty of Paris, it did not claim the Great Lakes region until 1787 with the creation of the Northwest Territory. The goal of the young nation was to gradually convert territories to states and establish settler, immigrant, refugee, and eventually freed slave ownership of the land. In 1800, Milwaukee became part of the Indiana Territory and in 1836 was included in the newly formed Wisconsin Territory, which in 1848 became the State of Wisconsin as we know it today.

The 1825 Treaty of Prairie du Chien established boundaries between the Indigenous communities in Wisconsin and removed the Ho-Chunk from their land in Milwaukee. The 1831 treaty with the Menominee ended their claim to lands they had been living on in Milwaukee, and the 1833 Treaty of Chicago cleared the way for the United States to attempt to forcibly relocate the Potawatomi from Milwaukee. The acts of war, coercion, and enslavement required to annihilate, remove, and attempt to assimilate the people living in this region are remembered by tribal nations today, and despite largely being forgotten by the greater public, continue to impact the Indigenous students, staff, and faculty at UWM.

For example, in 2020, UWM's Electa Quinney Institute for American Indian Education began working with Bader Philanthropies Inc. to create a space on campus dedicated to reconciliation. The resulting large fire circle designed by Chris Cornelius, an Oneida citizen and former associate professor in UWM's School of Architecture & Urban Planning, became a reality in October 2021, serving as a space for history to be remembered and relationships to be repaired for future generations. Many communities have given us words that speak clearly of the site where the fire circle is located and what that land means to them. In Ojibwe, the word "Minowaki" means "the Good Land," as does "Wēskōhsek" (now spelled "Wisconsin"), in Menominee. In Potawatomi, "Ménéwëk" refers to land where people had been living for many thousands of years that was then taken from them following an epic battle.

The long history of Indigenous people in Milwaukee was not included in the curriculum used by Catharine Beecher, who came to Milwaukee in 1851 to launch the Beecher Plan for educating women at the Milwaukee Normal Institute and High School (later Milwaukee College), which merged with Downer College in 1895 to become Milwaukee Downer College. Yet today the UWM fire circle sits outside Merrill, Johnston, and Holton Halls, constructed between 1897 and 1905 on what was then the Milwaukee Downer campus under the leadership of President Ellen Sabin. Although Beecher opposed President Andrew Jackson's Indian Removal Bill of 1830, and Sabin and her successors wanted the best for all Americans, like many other educators they believed in forced assimilation through schooling. Indeed, the United States continued to operate Indian boarding schools, divide Indigenous lands through allotment (Dawes Act of 1887), terminate Indigenous nations (the Menominee in 1954), and outlaw the teaching of Indigenous languages (until the Native American Languages Act of 1990)—all of which explains the limited participation in higher education among Indigenous people in Milwaukee.

In fact, it was not until 1969, during the American Indian movement, that Indigenous people began to exert control over their own education. In Milwaukee, three Oneida mothers took action after becoming frustrated with the lack of attention, growing problems, and low academic

▲

*Dorothy LePage, the first director of the Indian Community School, in her office, 1977.*
Photo courtesy Indian Community School.

performance their children were experiencing in the Milwaukee Public Schools. Marge Funmaker, Darlene Funmaker Neconish, and Marj Stevens organized and held classes, initially in one of their homes and later in the basement of the Church of All People. In August 1971, the women moved the school to the abandoned US Coast Guard station located on Milwaukee's lakefront after members of the Milwaukee chapter of the American Indian movement staged a takeover of the property, claiming it should be returned to the Indigenous people of the area from whom so much had been taken. This became the third home of the Indian Community School, originally funded through community donations and revenue from both state and federal offices of education. In 1970, Dorothy LePage, a Menominee student completing her degree in education at UWM, arranged to do her practicum at the new school. Following her graduation, LePage became the school's first director.

The school would move three more times between 1980 and 2007, facing financial hardships that caused it to close its doors for three years. Through perseverance and hard work, the school purchased land in Milwaukee and established trust status with the Forest County Potawatomi. This agreement, unheard of for its time, created an Indian gaming enterprise that not only provided a steady income stream to fund the school's

*The Indian Community School, 2022.* Photo courtesy Indian Community School.

operation, but also construction of its community building. In 2007, the Indian Community School opened its doors in Franklin, situated on more than two hundred acres of land filled with wildlife, wetlands, ponds, woods, medicinal plants, and other outdoor learning spaces for students.

The school is still attended by Milwaukee-area children with ties to a number of American Indian nations. Many of the school's graduates go on to earn high school diplomas and attend UWM, with some becoming teachers and school administrators in the Milwaukee area, thereby continuing the cycle of Indigenous control of their people's education.

American Indian Studies at UWM owes its existence primarily to a group of students who believed in the promise of education for Indigenous people and who in 1970 began demanding that UWM's administration support their goals. John Gauthier (Menominee), Lois Hall (LCO Ojibwe), James LaGoo (Bad River Ojibwe), and Jesse Torres (Oneida) were among the Indigenous students who saw education as a way to address poverty, strengthen tribal nations, and support Indigenous cultures. They formed organizations, wrote letters to editors, travelled to Madison and Washington, DC in search of funds for a program in American Indian studies, brought in nationally recognized Indigenous speakers, and organized conferences and pow wows.

In the late 1960s and early 1970s, such activism was responsible for important structural changes in the university's academic programs and highlighted the need to support Black, Latinx, and Indigenous students. The activism of the United Black Student Front and the Black Student Union, for example, led to the creation of the Center for Afro-American Studies in 1969, and the activist leadership of Roberto Hernández in 1970 brought about the formation of the Spanish Speaking Outreach Institute. Similarly, a group of community leaders, believing that change would occur only if Indigenous people themselves addressed the social issues caused by colonization and settlement, formed the American Indian Information and Action Group in a storefront in Milwaukee's central city in 1969. According to oral history, this group included Loretta Domencich, Marilyn "Mindimoye" Skenandore, Dave Lavadure, and Bill Kelly. In addition to providing a space for Indigenous people to gather and socialize, the organization worked with youth, offered reentry assistance to former inmates, and challenged governmental policies that were detrimental to tribal nations.

The following spring, at UWM, Gauthier and LaGoo formed an American Indian student union, which just months later was renamed the Native American Student Movement (NASM), with Professor of Anthropology Nancy Lurie as its faculty advisor. Five of the eight other Indigenous students on campus responded to an ad in the *UWM Post* recruiting members. The group went on to make news with its public demonstrations that included a march across campus that ended in a confrontation involving armed campus police outside the office of the chancellor. It was through such efforts that Indigenous people, though few in number at UWM, became visible for the first time on campus.

In October 1970, Assistant Chancellor for Student Services and Special Programs Ernest Spaights and Vice-Chancellor Lynn Eley visited the office of the American Indian Information and Action Group to discuss the possibility of an American Indian outreach program at UWM. Initial plans called for hiring student workers to recruit Indigenous students to the university, finding space on campus for NASM, and hiring a staff person to focus on student retention. That December, true to his word, Spaights offered Waldo "Buck" Martin, a Stockbridge-Munsee Mohican working as a homeschool coordinator in the Wisconsin Dells School District, a position in the highly successful Experimental Program in Higher Education (EPHE) as administrator of what Spaights was calling "the proposed Indian Student Program." (Today known as UWM's Pathway Advisory Program, EPHE was created in 1967 to recruit disadvantaged students with academic potential to UWM.) What's more, NASM was allocated physical space and a visible presence on campus, occupying a house at 3261 N. Maryland Ave. (currently, the location of the School of Architecture & Urban Planning) that it shared with the Spanish Speaking Outreach Institute.

At the urging of Spaights, NASM members began working toward consensus on elements of a program in American Indian studies, writing their suggestions on a blackboard in their new offices and revising the language until they had created a document describing an initiative that would largely come to fruition in subsequent years. The proposal addressed the recruitment

and retention of Indigenous students, academic offerings designed to address their specific needs, and courses (on religion, philosophy, politics, law, education, and history) designed to educate the larger UWM and Milwaukee communities about the history and culture of Indigenous peoples. The program proposal also envisioned an advisory committee comprised of students, faculty, and community members; outlined staff requirements that included not only a director but also support personnel; and called for a $50,000 annual budget.

On February 16, 1971, Spaights wrote to Chancellor J. Martin Klotsche, among others, seeking approval for NASM's "Proposal for a Native American Student Program at the UWM" (among administrators, sometimes referred to—and not always kindly, given the controversy it raised—

▲

*Waldo "Buck" Martin, the first coordinator of UWM's Native American Studies program.* Photo by Sharon Vanorny.

as the "Spaights Indian Proposal"), which had been developed by Martin, Lurie, and a group of Indigenous students. Consideration of the proposal at all levels moved quickly. Two days later, Vice-Chancellor William L. Walters directed Dean of the College of Letters and Science Howard J. Pincus to identify existing and potential courses for areas outlined in NASM's proposal, writing that "the main thing at this point is staff's capability to offer these courses and the overall sentiment toward such a cooperative effort."

Pincus, in turn, asked Associate Dean William F. Halloran to contact the departmental chairs in the College of Letters and Science for information about potential courses in American Indian studies, and asked Assistant Dean Donn K. Haglund to solicit commentary and assessments of the proposal from the university's four associate deans. For the most part, the department chairs and associate deans responded favorably to the proposal, although there was some notable dissent. One department chair, for example, expressed his disdain with a short note: "Faculty qualified to teach or interested in Native American Studies: NONE." Most others, however, and especially those in anthropology, geography, and history, took the exercise seriously. By late May, Halloran had identified nineteen existing courses that would support a program in American Indian studies and more than a dozen potential courses in fields such as linguistics, English, botany, and political science.

Halloran and Associate Dean Herman Weil expressed support for the proposal, but also noted concerns about the capacity of UWM's faculty to staff a program in American Indian studies. Weil pointed out that the proposal included a clear set of objectives, advice on offering courses on American Indian studies through seminars and independent study, and a "good" interdisciplinary curriculum and administrative structure. But Weil also noted that because funds had not been allocated for new courses or seminars, departments would be unable to pay faculty members to take on additional teaching responsibilities. Halloran expressed concern that UWM lacked "the faculty resources at this time to carry out the academic component." He suggested focusing on the recruitment and retention of Indigenous students, with the academic component implemented at a later date, an approach he said had been taken with "the Afro-American and Latin-American programs." In an anonymous, handwritten note, another associate dean agreed that the College of Letters and Science could identify courses for a program in American Indian studies, but warned that it should not "overtax" itself, writing that "it's easy for Spaights to put things on paper when somebody else has to deliver."

On July 1, 1971, Martin began working in EPHE, bringing a knowledge of Indigenous peoples and their issues, good humor, and enormous energy to the work of creating both an academic program and a support system for Indigenous students. Although he and NASM members continued to advocate for the new program, they saw little or no progress, reinforcing the notion that when it came to the development of ethnic studies programs, the accepted approach by UWM's administration was one of delay.

In October, in a sharply worded letter, NASM demanded that UWM fulfill its promises from the previous year, arguing that a budget-minded first step in creating a program in American Indian studies would be to consolidate all staff and initiatives involving Indigenous people under one banner. Without proper coordination, the writers asserted, attempts to support American Indian studies remained "frustratingly uncoordinated, piece-meal, and half-hearted." The letter suggested that Martin, in his new position, was just "an ordinary EPHE counselor," whereas, if he were named administrator of a formal program in American Indian studies, he could be "scouting Indian faculty, seeking sources of funds to assist students and the program generally, working with departments through which courses might be implemented." The letter also suggested making Josephine Bigler (Yuchi), who was working in UWM's Office of Admissions, a staff member in American Indian studies. Lastly, NASM members reminded UWM administrators that Indian students had waited two years for action and pointed out that although UWM established other ethnic studies programs in the wake of "aggressive pressure and hostility," they preferred to take a less combative approach.

The letter had some effect. On November 1, Martin was assigned to the College of Letters and Science's Office of Scholastic Affairs, raising his profile as well as prospects for a program in American Indian studies. Unfortunately, Martin was now responsible not only for recruiting, advising, and supporting Indigenous students, but also myriad other tasks: working on potential course offerings and fundraising related to a program in American Indian studies, representing the college on Indigenous issues involving other campus units and other universities across the state, developing relationships with the Milwaukee Indigenous community, and acting as a liaison with other UWM ethnic studies programs.

American Indian studies faced yet another obstacle when on February 21, 1972, Klotsche announced a moratorium on the creation of new graduate or undergraduate programs at UWM. Lurie argued that UWM was in a unique position to be the first campus in the UW System to "capture Indian studies," while also noting that such a program was not technically "new" given Martin's hiring. In addition, Lurie emphasized that budget cuts and other financial restraints should not negate prior commitments made to recruit, retain, and support Indigenous students. She pointed out that UWM had an opportunity to establish a strong program, in large part because it could draw from Milwaukee, where most Indigenous people in the state resided. Lurie also proposed that UWM add a series of courses on Indigenous issues to the regular curriculum and develop outreach programs to urban Indigenous populations aimed at alleviating poverty and cultural loss.

UWM's Native American Studies Program (NASP) finally launched in spring 1972, with Martin as the nascent unit's coordinator and only staff member. By that fall, UWM was offering three courses through NASP: Red Power & Contemporary Indian Issues, Native American World Views, and Native American Music. (As was often the case in the early years of the program, these courses were taught by non-Indigenous faculty and Indigenous lecturers holding temporary appointments.) Meanwhile, Martin managed to attract new students to UWM. Consider, for example, that in 1970, when John Gauthier began discussions about the possibility of a program in American Indian studies, fewer than ten students identified as Indigenous; however, by sometime in 1972, more than sixty Indigenous students were enrolled at UWM.

Martin also identified two other issues that were—and continue to be—crucial to Indigenous students and Indigenous peoples: heath care and language. In June, Martin submitted a proposal

and budget to establish a path for Indigenous students to find careers in the health field, citing both the vital need for such care in Indigenous communities and the need for Indigenous health care professionals. Despite initial interest, this initiative appears not to have moved forward. Martin, however, did find long-term success with a project on the teaching of Indigenous languages. He understood the social, cultural, and religious importance of language to Indigenous communities, and—having worked in Wisconsin public schools—recognized that proper instruction required excellent materials and well-trained instructors. As a result, he convinced the Great Lakes Inter-Tribal Council (GLITC), a consortium of Indigenous nations in Wisconsin and Michigan, to seek funds for language teaching and preservation through Title IV of the Indian Education Act. After securing a $510,480 federal language grant, GLITC subcontracted with UWM to develop such a program.

That initiative, the Wisconsin Native American Languages Program (WNALP) began in 1973, bringing together three professional linguists and twelve Indigenous speakers of Ojibwe (at the time, Chippewa), Potawatomi, Menominee, Oneida, and Ho-Chunk (at the time, Winnebago) to develop orthographies, dictionaries, grammars, and other teaching tools. John Beaudin (Ojibwe) stepped away from his studies at UWM to coordinate the program. (Beaudin later received his undergraduate degree from UW-Green Bay and a law degree from what was by then the University of Wisconsin–Madison.)

The materials developed through WNALP, a complete set of which can be found in UWM's Golda Meir Library, continue to be used today by Indigenous communities in language revitalization.

*Wallace Pyawasit (right), an Indigenous speaker in the Wisconsin Native American Languages program who went on to teach at UWM, with a student at a campus gathering, 1970s.*

16  **TELLING OUR STORIES:** A HISTORY OF DIVERSITY AT THE UNIVERSITY OF WISCONSIN-MILWAUKEE, **1956–2022**

They include Omāēqnomenēw-Kīketwanan: *An English-Menominee and Menominee-English Word List,* jointly published in 1975 by the Wisconsin Department of Public Instruction, GLITC, and UWM. In a 2006 research article about Potawatomi language revival strategies, Christopher Wetzel wrote that he found the curriculum materials developed by WNALP "in tribal headquarters and libraries across the United States, as well as individual homes."

The work the language speakers did through WNALP qualified them to receive state teaching certification, and many went on to apply their expertise. Hannah Maulson, for example, taught Anishinaabemowin (Ojibwemowin) to members of the Lac du Flambeau Band of the Lake Superior Chippewa Indians, and Maria Hinton, considered a founder of the Oneida Nation School System, assisted in the revitalization of the Oneida language for the Oneida Nation of Wisconsin. Hinton—along with her brother Amos Christjohn and linguist Clifford Abbott—authored *An Oneida Dictionary: Ukwehu wehneha Tekawanate?nyése,* in 1996. What's more, three of the Indigenous speakers in WNALP later went on to teach at UWM: Wallace Pyawasit (Menominee), Bill Daniels Jr. (Forest County Potawatomi), and Emily Schwamp (Oneida). Pyawasit enjoyed a long and congenial relationship with UWM and its students, and at the time of his death, the Indigenous community on campus—saddened to lose the only Indigenous language-speaker on campus—created an award in his name to honor outstanding Indigenous leaders in the Milwaukee community.

Meanwhile, in January 1973, John Boatman, previously the administrative assistant to Congressman Alvin O'Konski and an ad hoc instructor, had been hired as an academic specialist to assist Martin and to teach one NASP course. An Ojibwe from Marinette, Wisconsin, Boatman had earned his master's degree from UWM in sociology. In a handwritten note to Associate Dean Ron Snyder in March, Boatman wrote, "I know this might be considered Utopian, but I have waited since 1958 for an opportunity to write something like this for UWM," referring to a fifteen-page document (including two appendices and a budget) that spelled out the rationale for a suitably funded program based on the three areas first outlined by NASM years before: an

academic course of study serving both Indigenous and non-Indigenous students, recruitment and support of Indigenous students, and outreach to the Indigenous Milwaukee community. Boatman argued that the first two areas were largely unsupported, noting that UWM employed only one Indigenous instructor, Roger Thomas (Bad River Oijbwe), and no tenure-track faculty. He noted as well that although the number of Indigenous students enrolled for the 1972–1973 academic year had grown to 110, Martin alone could not reasonably be expected to support seventy-five students, given the unique circumstances of Indigenous students.

Boatman's assessment mirrored points made in NASM's earlier program proposal, noting for example, that as many as one-third of Wisconsin's Indigenous population (approximately twenty-five thousand individuals) lived in Milwaukee, representing a potential source of students who, if enrolled, would help diversify the campus. Boatman also pointed out that because of the historically contentious relationship between Indigenous nations and the US government, Indigenous students experienced unique needs. He argued, for instance, that Indigenous peoples were, in effect, "prisoners of war in their own country," referencing US policies allowing the annexation of vast, state-sized swaths of Indigenous lands and the monetization of Indigenous natural resources, as well as the subsequent blame placed on Indigenous people for their poverty. Boatman maintained that NASP needed staff members who, like Martin, were willing to visit potential Indigenous students in their homes as part of the recruitment process as a way to "break down the walls of suspicion that dissuade those potential students form the higher education enterprise." (Such suspicion can be traced to the attitudes of Indian boarding school officials who sought to use education to destroy the cultures of Indigenous peoples—officials such as Captain Richard Henry Pratt, superintendent of the first Indian boarding school, who famously declared in 1892, "kill the Indian . . . and save the man.") In other words, Boatman suggested, without an Indigenous culture within the university, NASP's future would be limited.

In his analysis, Boatman set targets for the number of faculty and staff members hired and the number of courses offered, describing the

natural alliances between American Indian studies and the disciplines of anthropology, history, the arts, and literature. He identified groups and organizations with a stake in the program, such as NASM and Milwaukee-area organizations serving Indigenous people, and suggested ways for these groups to meet with UWM officials in financial aid, admissions, and counseling services to help develop the new program and ensure the success of Indigenous students. He communicated the importance of dedicated space for Indigenous students to gather, socialize, and create their own home within the larger university community. Finally, Boatman noted that the program should be assessed not only on data related to recruitment, retention, and academic achievement, but also on input from Indigenous communities. Here again, Boatman was pointing out that it was not enough for UWM to admit and support Indigenous students; it was also necessary for Indigenous people to have a voice in shaping their presence on campus.

Boatman's clear and compelling analysis of NASP almost immediately shifted the degree of UWM's commitment to the program. Associate

Dean Nason E. Hall, in a letter to Vice-Chancellor William L. Walters, described the needs of NASP as far outpacing its proposed budget. What's more, Hall went on to cite three reasons why a robust, financially secure NASP was important to UWM: it would "demonstrate UWM's recognition of Native Americans as an important constituency"; encourage Indigenous peoples to attend universities, perhaps helping to mitigate some of the historically negative associations between American educational systems and Indigenous peoples; and demonstrate that American Indian studies was a legitimate field useful to Indigenous and non-Indigenous peoples—particularly non-Indigenous students going into fields where they were "likely to work closely with Native American residents in Wisconsin." And in April, Snyder and Hall named Boatman NASM coordinator—a position he would occupy for the next thirty-two years. Martin, poised to leave UWM the following summer to attend graduate school in Washington state, was made responsible for student recruitment, advising, support, and retention.

By the fall of 1973, the number of Indigenous students at UWM had reached 145. The following year, that number rose to 154, and over the next 15 years, averaged 133. Upon Martin's departure, Boatman hired Sue Chicks-Wojciechowski (Stockbridge-Munsee), a graduate of UWM's School of Social Welfare, to assume responsibility for Indigenous student services, and Diane Ogimaa-giizhigokwe Amour (Prairie Band Pottawatomi) to work as a tutor. Amour, who would go on to spend the next forty years at UWM, including thirty as coordinator of the American Indian Student Services Office, was a 2020 recipient of an Ernest Spaights Plaza Award in recognition of her significant contributions to the university and the community.

Boatman would find developing the academic component of NASP particularly challenging. In his initial attempt to bring Indigenous faculty to UWM, Boatman wrote to a number of nationally renowned Indigenous scholars in the country—academics such as N. Scott Momaday, Dee Brown, and Henrietta Whiteman—all of whom had attended conferences at UWM. Boatman asked each to consider joining the faculty, but he was unable to draw them to Milwaukee. For the next few years, Boatman relied on mostly Indigenous lecturers and some Indigenous graduate students to sustain the academics of the program. They included Edward Wapp (Comanche and Sac & Fox), to teach Native American Music: Great Lakes Region, and Thomas, at the time a UWM PhD student in anthropology, to teach Native American World Views and Anishinaabemowin (Ojibwemowin) language classes. (Following his years at UWM, Wapp became an instructor at the Institute of American Indian Arts in Santa Fe, New Mexico.) Boatman, meanwhile, developed and taught courses on Indigenous subjects in the Departments of Sociology, Philosophy, and Anthropology.

*Kimberly M. Blaeser, professor of English and Wisconsin Poet Laureate from 2015 to 2016, was awarded the 2021 Lifetime Achievement Award from the Native Writers' Circle of the Americas.*

*Former Associate Professor of Anthropology Bernard C. Perley, currently an affiliated faculty member at the Electa Quinney Institute.*

In fall 1974, Boatman hired the first tenure-track Indigenous faculty member at UWM, Silvester Brito-Hunting Bear (Comanche and Purépecha), who received a joint appointment in English and anthropology. Soon after, Ron Lewis (Cherokee) joined the faculty of what was then the School of Social Welfare, becoming the first tenured Indigenous person in the UW System. Yet these early successes were short lived, with budget limitations the main obstacle in bringing more Indigenous tenure-track faculty to UWM. Over the years, Boatman went to different departments and offered to pay one-half or one-fourth of a potential candidate's salary from his limited budget as an incentive to recruit and hire Indigenous faculty. He wrote of having an excellent working relationship with the Department of Sociology, Department of Philosophy, Department of Botany, and especially the Department of History, which sought and hired Indigenous historians entirely with its own departmental funds. Meanwhile, some Indigenous faculty were unable to earn tenure, while others—including Lewis, JoAllyn Archambault (Standing Rock Sioux), Don Fixico

(Shawnee, Sac & Fox, Muscogee Creek and Seminole), Duane Champagne (Turtle Mountain Ojibwe), and Tom Holm (Plains Cherokee)—stayed for a short time at UWM before taking positions elsewhere. Wrote Boatman in 1985, "Unfortunately, because of the lack of faculty positions and funds, we have not been able to make any significant progress in this area."

In 1986, the program changed considerably when NASP was divided into two separate units, eventually named American Indian Studies, headed by Boatman, and American Indian Student Services (AISS) in the College of Letters and Science's Office of Central Advising, coordinated by Amour. In 1987, Boatman facilitated the hiring of Donald Green (Chickasaw) in sociology, Kimberly M. Blaeser (White Earth Anishinaabe) in English, Anton Treuer (White Earth Ojibwe) and Cary Miller (Saint Croix Ojibwe) in history, and Bernard C. Perley (Malaseet) in anthropology—faculty who provided stability in the program for years to come. Boatman would continue in his position until his retirement in 2002, when the role of director of the American Indian Studies program became an elected position among the Indigenous faculty—a role most often, and currently, held by Associate Professor of English Michael Wilson (Choctaw Nation of Oklahoma). Wilson's teaching and research interests include Indigenous literatures of North America and postcolonial theory.

Professor Michael Wilson lecturing on American Indian history, 2018. Photo by Chia Youyee Vang.

In 1999, through a gift from the Indian Community School to UWM, both the academic and student support units were bolstered by the creation of the Electa Quinney Institute for American Indian Education. The institute is named for Electa Quinney, Wisconsin's first public school teacher and a member of Wisconsin's Stockbridge-Munsee band of Mohicans. Trained in New York and Connecticut, Quinney came to Wisconsin in 1827 following the removal of her community from the area that is now New York State. The year after her arrival, Quinney founded the state's first school without an enrollment fee in Kaukauna, where she taught American Indian, settler, and immigrant students, many of whom would not have been able to attend if school fees had been in place.

Directed first by David Beaulieu, a nationally recognized scholar of educational policy, and later by poet and linguist Margaret Noodin (Anishinaabe descent), the institute has been the recipient of grants totaling more than $9 million from the Office of Indian Education in the US Department of Education. These awards have to date supported, in the form of scholarships, more than thirty Indigenous students as they earned degrees to become certified teachers and licensed administrators in Wisconsin. The institute has also received funding to support Indigenous language revitalization and research driven by the needs and interests of Wisconsin's sovereign nations and Milwaukee's urban American Indian community.

Research led by the Electa Quinney Institute and its faculty affiliates often centers on Indigenous frameworks and methodologies. The institute is focused on partnering with native nations and maintaining visibility for Indigenous peoples and intellectual traditions. A significant concern is restoration and justice through legal avenues such as compliance with the Native American Graves Protection and Repatriation Act and education about sovereign treaty rights as required by Wisconsin Act 31.

Over the years, UWM has been home to a number of American Indian Ancestors whose remains came to campus as a result of archaeological excavations. The institute has played a role by helping the UWM community process the trauma of this reality and to heal by acknowledging direct connections between the past and present. Because it is unusual for humans to be held in such a way, there is a need to recognize and comfort the Ancestors whose remains are on our campus until they can possibly be returned to their sovereign nations.

Through the institute and the Indian Community School, students at UWM are able to access speakers of Indigenous languages and ensure that their revitalization continues. In 2021, for example, the Indigenous Languages of Wisconsin course enabled students to study Anishinaabemowin (Ojibwe, Potawatomi, and Odawa), Oneida, Menominee, or Ho-Chunk for credit and to satisfy second language learning requirements. Meanwhile, some of the first courses in American Indian Studies continue to be offered, including surveys in American Indian history, literature, and ethnobotany. Newer offerings include Contemporary Issues of the American Indian; System Failure: Globalization and Language Extinction; and American History, Law, and Government. Students can also participate in seminars, apprenticeships, and independent study. Partnerships with GLITC, the Gerald L. Ignace Indian Health Center of Milwaukee, and several tribal colleges have allowed the institute to increase the number of Indigenous students on campus and the amount of Indigenous-focused research undertaken at UWM.

What's more, UWM's American Indian Studies Certificate program provides students with a thorough understanding of the American Indian tribal nations in North America and their influence and impact in today's culture and society. The certificate, which is earned through a combination of courses in American Indian Studies and disciplines such as anthropology, English, history, and sociology, focuses on the Indigenous peoples of North America, how they were impacted by European explorers, and ways in which the two groups transformed each other. It complements a number of majors, making graduates more marketable for jobs that require an understanding of the American Indian population. Students earning the certificate often find themselves well prepared for jobs in areas ranging from business and education to government, politics, wildlife management, and health care. Some take positions on Indian reservations and at agencies such as the US Bureau of Indian Affairs, the US Bureau of Land Management, and the US Forestry Service. In order to obtain the certificate, students must maintain a minimum GPA of 2.5 and complete at least eighteen approved credits in the American Indian Studies program, including twelve that must be earned in residence at UWM.

Today, UWM's American Indian Studies program is home to five Indigenous faculty members and two Indigenous instructors;

▲

*Mishiikenh (Vern) Altiman overseeing the making of maple syrup over the Electa Quinney Institute's fire circle, March 2022.* Photo by David J. Pate Jr.

Indigenous student enrollment stands at 306. Additionally, in February 2022, following a national search, Joan Nesbitt (Cherokee) was appointed UWM's vice-chancellor for development and alumni relations—the first Indigenous individual to serve the university at that level.

UWM's 42nd Annual Autumn Pow Wow was held in November 2019, marking a time of feasting with relatives and the onset of storytelling season. In 2020, a pandemic paused this tradition, but several women in the community organized a virtual jingle dance in memory of the pandemic of 1918 and the many other times Indigenous communities had faced disease and needed healing. By fall 2021, with the arrival on campus of the grandfather stones for the fire circle, a group of students, staff, faculty, and community members gathered and danced together again. Their resiliency will always be a part of the UWM story.

CHAPTER 2

# Lifting Up the Race: The Contributions of Black Folk at UWM

David J. Pate Jr.,
H. Victoria Pryor, and
Derrick Vaughn Langston

*Brandon L. Savage receives his bachelor's degree in social work from the University of Wisconsin-Milwaukee (UWM), 2017. As a McNair Scholar, Savage researched the link between debt and incarceration of African American males.*

The history of the Black experience at the University of Wisconsin-Milwaukee (UWM) is rooted in more than six decades of efforts to recruit and retain Black faculty, staff, and students. Central to the story are scores of Black individuals renowned for their scholarship and skills who were committed to diversifying the campus and who, to that end, championed numerous initiatives that changed the lives not only of their peers, but also other people with racialized identities on campus. Nevertheless, as the data suggest, the challenge persists and the struggle is far from over.

In 1956, when the University of Wisconsin-Milwaukee (UWM) was established, "Negro" was the term used for people we today refer to as African American or Black. Ibram X. Kendi writes in *Four Hundred Souls: A Community History of African America 1619–2019* that the use of the descriptive word "African" speaks to a people of African descent. The term "Black" speaks to a people racialized as Black. Because race is a socially constructed phenomenon, Black is used to identify a wide array of people from a variety of countries. And although many of UWM's early Black faculty were descendants of enslaved Africans, others have come from countries such as the Democratic Republic of the Congo, Egypt, Ghana, Kenya, Nigeria, and Sierra Leone on the continent of Africa, and Haiti and Jamaica in the Caribbean.

According to the Wisconsin Department of Health Services, African Americans or Blacks have been present in Wisconsin since the 1700s when Black enslaved people were forced to work as fur traders, as farmers in Vernon and Grant counties, and as soldiers in the Civil War—specifically in the 29th Infantry Regiment, US Colored Troops. It was after slavery ended in 1865 that African Americans

began moving northward in search of a better life. However, the *Encyclopedia of Milwaukee* reports that it was "the late great migration" of Blacks to Milwaukee following World War II that brought large numbers of African Americans to Wisconsin. According to the Wisconsin Historical Society, the state's African American population increased nearly 600 percent—from 12,158 to 74,546—between 1940 and 1960. And between 1945 and 1960, notes historian John Gurda, the number of Milwaukee's Black residents increased from roughly 13,000 to 62,458.

Unfortunately, there is limited information available on UWM's first Black students. Black graduates pictured in the 1956 and 1957 editions of *The Ivy*, UWM's yearbook, are Geraldine Fowlkes; Henry Eugene Jefferson, a member of Kappa Alpha Psi fraternity; La Vera Laws; Melicent Tucker; and George Walker—all of whom majored in education. The first yearbook photo of a Black athlete was of R. Warren, a member of UWM's 1957 track team.

Korean War veteran and boxing champion Robert Harris Jr. received his bachelor's degree in elementary education in 1954 from Wisconsin State College, Milwaukee—one of UWM's predecessor institutions—where he was the first Black student admitted to the School of Education. Harris went on to teach, coach, and referee in the Milwaukee Public Schools and became the first Black high school basketball referee in the state of Wisconsin. He volunteered extensively in the community before enrolling at UWM, where he earned a master's degree in urban education in 1969. Harris became an enthusiastic supporter of his new alma mater. He served as a member of the UWM Alumni Association's Board of Trustees from 1994 to 2004; as founder and first president of the association's

African American Chapter in 1997; and as a member of the UWM Board of Visitors, an advisory group charged with raising awareness of the university, from 1998 to 2006. He also, for a time, worked at the university as an adjunct lecturer.

Information on Black faculty during the late 1950s and 1960s at UWM is also spotty; however, a few professors were known to be teaching in the departments of philosophy, political science, geography, and educational psychology. Cornelius Golightly, for example, was an assistant professor of philosophy at the University of Wisconsin Extension Division in Milwaukee in 1955, the year before the Extension Division merged with Wisconsin State College, Milwaukee to form UWM. Golightly assumed the same position at UWM the following year, becoming the Department of Philosophy's first Black faculty member. In 1959, Golightly was promoted to associate professor (he would be made a full professor in 1965) and granted tenure, making him the first Black faculty member to receive tenure in the University of Wisconsin System. In 1961, Golightly became the first African American to win election to the Milwaukee School Board, where he fought to introduce busing to integrate city schools. In 1966, he was appointed director of UWM's Summer Sessions, making him the first African American to hold a major administrative post at the university. Golightly left UWM in 1969 when he was appointed an associate dean and professor of philosophy at Wayne State University.

Lucius J. Barker, hired as an instructor professor of political science in 1956, rose through the ranks to become an assistant professor in 1958 and an associate professor in 1962. He became a

In 1954, Robert Harris Jr. was the first Black student admitted to the School of Education at Wisconsin State College, Milwaukee, one of UWM's predecessor institutions. Harris later earned a master's degree in urban education from UWM and became one of the university's strongest supporters.

Cornelius Golightly became the first Black faculty member in UWM's Department of Philosophy in 1956.

leading scholar on the political implications of race, civil liberties, and the judicial system. His book, *Civil Liberties and the Constitution*—coauthored with his brother Twiley W. Barker and now in its ninth edition—is considered the classic textbook on the structure of the American legal system. Barker left UWM in 1967 to accept an assistant chancellor position at the University of Illinois; he went on to chair the political science departments at both Washington University in St. Louis, and Stanford University.

In a 1991 oral interview, Barker remembered UWM in its first years as a "newly developing campus" and "an urban university for the most part" that "did a heck of a lot almost exclusively." Continued Barker, "Now, since [then], it's become a very big institution. . . . [But] I saw it from its infancy. . . . I enjoyed it very much."

Harold M. Rose received a joint appointment in the Department of Geography and Department of Urban Affairs in 1962. One of the first tenured Black professors at the university, Rose had begun his career exploring issues related to natural resource management. However, after arriving in Milwaukee, Rose shifted his focus, engaging in pioneering research on the conditions faced by Blacks in Milwaukee and building a national reputation on the ways racism and racial policy affected urbanization. Rose is also credited with creating and developing the field of urban geography.

In 1995, the same year he retired, Rose was named a UWM Distinguished Professor, certainly one of the first—if not the very first—of the university's Black scholars to be so recognized.

▲

▲

*Lucius J. Barker, who joined the faculty of UWM's Department of Political Science in 1956, became a leading scholar on the political implications of race, civil liberties, and the judicial system.*
Photo courtesy Stanford University.

*Distinguished Professor Emeritus of Geography and Urban Studies Harold M. Rose, who became an expert on the conditions faced by Blacks in Milwaukee, was one of the first tenured Black professors at UWM.*

renowned civil rights leader and activist. It later evolved into the Sullivan-Spaights Professorship. Today it is known as the Sullivan-Spaights Endowment and is held by Associate Professor of Social Work David J. Pate Jr.) In 2001, a Sullivan-Spaights Scholarship was created for full-time, underrepresented minority students from the Milwaukee Public Schools who demonstrated community leadership.

Spaights also served as a special assistant to the chancellor for educational opportunity and as an assistant chancellor in charge of student services and special programs. The Ernest Spaights Plaza Award, presented in recognition of "significant, enduring, and institution-wide contributions to the university," was established in his name in 1993. In 1994, Golightly was one of the first such individuals recognized with the award.

It must be acknowledged that there was a dearth of female professors—and no Black female professors—at UWM prior 1971, a time when university professorships were primarily seen as

The Department of Geography, in 2014, established the Harold M. Rose Lecture Series, with a focus on race and urban social justice, in tribute to his legacy. Although the series is no longer ongoing, in 2018, Michigan State University Professor of Geography Joe T. Darden came to campus to lecture on "Understanding Harold Rose's Geography of Despair: The persistence of the black ghetto and neighborhood socioeconomic inequality." Finally, the American Association of Geographers established what is now the Harold M. Rose Award for Anti-Racism Research and Practice in Geography in 2012 "to honor geographers who have advanced the discipline through their research on racism, and who have also had an impact on anti-racist practice."

Ernest Spaights began his long and distinguished career at UWM when he was hired in 1965 as an assistant professor in the Department of Educational Psychology. Spaights served both the School of Education and what was then the School of Social Welfare, holding the Sullivan Professorship from 1979, when it was established, to 1991. (The professorship was created to honor the Reverend Leon Howard Sullivan, a nationally

*Ernest Spaights, professor of education and social work and special assistant to Chancellor J. Martin Klotsche, was instrumental in recruiting underrepresented and disadvantaged students to UWM.*

▶

United Black Student Front members at a press conference in Chapman Hall on March 1, 1969, demanding that the university's Center for Afro-American Culture be given degree-granting authority. The students include (left to right): George Walker, Earl Barney (reading), Jerry Belin (standing in back), Barbara Garrison, Enis Ragland, and Larry Barnett (second from right).

positions for white males. That said, the issue of inclusion and equity became a prominent topic of discussion in the 1960s, with students across the country demanding access and recognition, and calling on university administrators to increase the number of Black students, staff, and faculty on their campuses.

The story was no different at UWM, where in response to such demands Chancellor J. Martin Klotsche charged Spaights with recruiting underrepresented and disadvantaged students and hiring personnel to support their efforts. One of Spaights's earliest such initiatives, created in 1967, was UWM's Experimental Program for Higher Education (EPHE). As described by UWM doctoral candidate Akbar Ally in his 1981 dissertation *Equal Opportunities Programs for Black Students in Public Urban Universities: A Case Study,* "EPHE provided an opportunity for low-income minority and disadvantaged students to receive higher education," by functioning as a gateway through which students "from any ethnic background who did not meet the statutory requirements for regular admissions" could be admitted to UWM. EPHE, which operated out of the Division of Student Services and Special Programs, served six students in its first year—a number that would grow to more than thirteen hundred per year by the end of the decade.

Indeed, the 1960s became a time of reckoning for those seeking civil rights and equal access to the American dream for all. On campuses across America—including UWM—Black students were demanding social justice in terms of increased access and recognition. Consider, for example, the following series of events that led to the university's first foray into African American studies, as documented in the UWM Libraries' timeline of African American student activism and other archival materials and Ally's dissertation:

○ — In May 1968, the United Black Student Front (UBSF) presented Klotsche with a list of demands that included creation of a Black Student Union (BSU) led by a policy-making board composed of minority faculty, staff, and students that would administer a formal program in African American studies focused on "preparation in fields directly related to our own lives and especially designed to better prepare us to improve our lives and the welfare of our people." Klotsche's promise to explore various options did not satisfy the group, prompting a press conference and intervention by Spaights and four other African American faculty members.

— On June 3, 1968, the UWM Faculty Senate approved the formation of an ad hoc committee to create a Center for Afro-American Culture (CAAC). Apparently in deference to the students, the senate voted to create the BSU by September.

— In February 1969, a group of fifty African American students met with Klotsche to demand that James Turner, a lecturer in anthropology, be considered for appointment as CAAC director. Following the meeting, they joined another two hundred students to rally and then march across campus in support of Turner.

— On March 1, 1969, Turner and a group of students met again with Klotsche, presenting him with a series of demands that included making CAAC a degree-granting university unit, a move the ad hoc committee rejected two weeks later. The BSU subsequently withdrew its support for the CAAC, announcing that "they would no longer support any type of African-American Studies programs created by the faculty and the university."

— On July 31, 1969, Daniel Burrell, a Milwaukee community organizer strongly supported by Spaights, accepted the position of director of the CAAC.

— On December 6, 1969, the University of Wisconsin Board of Regents approved Klotsche's proposal for a permanent Center for Afro-American Studies, one of the first two such programs in the United States.

— On July 1, 1971, the Center for Afro-American Studies became the Department of Afro-American Studies in the College of Letters and Science.

According to UWM officials, the CAAC was designed "to support Black students' adaptation to UWM, to serve as a mediator between the black community of Milwaukee and the university, and to play a role in the development of the field of Black studies locally, regionally and internationally." No doubt, it also contributed to the increase in the number of Black undergraduates at UWM, which between 1968 and 1979 jumped from 240 to 1,307.

# ALPHA PHI ALPHA
## SOCIAL FRATERNITY

*The founding members of the Epsilon Tau Chapter of Alpha Phi Alpha fraternity. Front row: Gene Oliver, Carl Nevels, and Will Kirk. Back row: Milton Coleman, John Huettner (advisor), and Thomas Smith.*

Even prior to the Jim Crow era and the civil rights movement, race was the central point of social interaction in the United States, determining not only those with whom Blacks could socialize or live, but also defining their sense of belonging. And indeed, in the 1960s, race and Black identity continued to be a social organizing factor, even on college campuses. Nine Black Greek organizations, collectively known as The Divine Nine, had come into existence across the country beginning in 1906 to deal with this issue—specifically by providing Black college students with the opportunity to socialize exclusively with each other while on campus. The first of these Black organizations UWM formally recognized and made eligible for university funding was Alpha Phi Alpha fraternity, in 1964. Ultimately, three more Black Greek organizations would also be chartered on the UWM campus: Alpha Kappa Alpha sorority (1974); Omega Psi Phi fraternity (1978); and Sigma Gamma Rho sorority

(1980). Two others—Kappa Alpha Psi fraternity (1954) and Delta Sigma Theta sorority (1973)—were created in Milwaukee under citywide charters.

As they did across the country, these Greek organizations gave Black UWM students their first chance to socialize, reside together in university housing, and enjoy a sense of belonging without judgment. One of the early members of Alpha Phi Alpha was Milton Coleman, who pledged UWM's Epsilon Tau Chapter of Alpha Phi Alpha in spring 1964 and was initiated the following summer, making him one of the fraternity's first five members. (Lucius J. Barker was also a member of Alpha Phi Alpha and thus eligible to be the group's original advisor. The subsequent faculty advisor was John Huettner, who was not a member of the fraternity.)

Coleman, who would go on to earn a bachelor's of fine arts degree in music history and literature from UWM in 1968, has enjoyed a distinguished career in journalism, which began at the *Milwaukee Courier,* Wisconsin's oldest Black-owned newspaper. Coleman then worked for forty years at the *Washington Post,* rising to the post of senior editor. He also served as president of the Inter American Press Association and the American Society of News Editors. In 2012, he was named the first University of Wisconsin-Milwaukee Foundation Alumni Fellow, a tribute designed to recognize "eminent alumni who have achieved leadership and accomplishment in their fields." At the time, Coleman told the *UWM Report* that he credited his college years for his success, noting that "I could not have had a more intellectually stimulating educational, civic and social experience than the one I received at UW. I left campus well equipped to compete with the

*Joan M. Prince earned four degrees from UWM and served as one of the university's top administrators for more than twenty years.* Photo by Troye Fox.

*Gary L. Williams, associate professor emeritus in the Department of Educational Policy and Community Studies and founder and director of UWM's Institute for Intercultural Research.* Photo by Troye Fox.

best and was ultimately blessed with opportunities to be a leader among them."

Joan M. Prince, a member of Delta Sigma Theta sorority, earned four degrees from UWM: a bachelor's of arts in 1977, a bachelor's in medical technology in 1982, a master's of science in 1992, and a PhD in urban education in 1999. She recalled the university as "a microcosm of our region, our city, and our state." Continued Prince, who would go on to serve for more than twenty years as one of UWM's top administrators, "Everything that was happening outside of the institution was brought into the institution. So, when I walked onto campus I sometimes was welcomed with open arms, but other times—based on race—arms were closed."

Gary L. Williams, associate professor emeritus of education, spent more than fifty years at UWM, where he earned a bachelor's degree in sociology in 1975, a master's degree in political science in 1977, and a PhD in urban studies in 1991, and served as an associate professor in the Department of Educational Policy and Community Studies. Williams also was the founder, in 2002, and longtime director of the university's Institute for Intercultural Research. A member of Alpha Phi Alpha fraternity, Williams could identify with the students he encountered during the 1980s and 1990s, noting that he and other Black faculty and staff members "felt it was our responsibility to let these students know that we cared about their success in school so we would often go to the meeting space where the students congregated." Williams—then director of UWM's Student Support Services—recalled that he and his colleagues knew the students' schedules and would "remind them that they should be in class at that

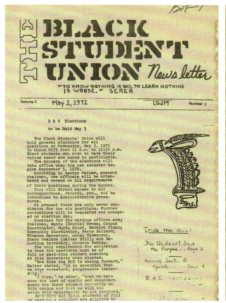

*The* Black Critic, *September 1972.*

*The* Black Student Union Newsletter, *May 1, 1972.*

Invictus, *November 2, 1977.*

time and that they were here to learn, not simply socialize. . . ."

Members of both Black social and activist organizations had been meeting together at various locations on and near campus since the 1960s. For example, an informal group known as Soul Place—the precursor to the BSU—held its meetings in rented space at Kenwood Methodist Church on Milwaukee's East Side. Other meeting spots where Black students felt a sense of inclusion were located in the UWM Student Union, and commonly referred to as "The Pit" and "Third Street." And from 1981 to 1984 in Sandburg Hall, a gathering spot known as the Cabaret dedicated Thursday nights to Black students and their music, presented by a Black disc jockey.

Among the faculty and staff there were a number who, according to Williams, took their role as what he called "pseudo parents" particularly seriously, treating the Black students as members of their families. They included Susan Fields, program manager for African American Student Academic Services (AASAS) from 1979 to 2015, and Diana V. Edwards, who in 1982 became the first African American advisor in the office of Black Student Advising. In 2019, AASAS merged with the Black Cultural Center—created in 2009 to promote outreach to, and the retention and graduation of African American students—to form the Black

Student Cultural Center (BSCC). According to its website, the center's goal is to "serve as a resource for students of African descent by partnering with UWM units and departments, community organizations and local businesses." Edwards, who remained in her post until 2013, recalled that "back in the day" she would personally walk Black students she found socializing in the Student Union to class, telling them, "You don't need to be sitting here on 3rd Street."

Meanwhile, a number of BSU publications, including the *Black Critic* and the *Black Student Union Newsletter*, were chronicling the Black experience at UWM and the surrounding community. According to the UWM Libraries' Digital Collections, the *Black Critic* was "short-lived due to lack of support and resources, but it stood as a foundation for Invictus, the longest running of the Black Student Union publications." *Invictus* was published intermittently from 1977 to 1995, and included a mix of news, feature stories and poetry. The *Black Student Voice,* published in 1993, led to a "relaunch" of *Invictus* during the 1994–1995 academic year—a move designed to position the publication as a "third leg between the left-leaning *UWM Post* and the right-leaning *UWM Times*."

Also popular among Blacks on campus was the evening radio talk show *Rapport Afro American* that originally aired six days a week—and later just on Sundays—on WUWM, originally UWM's student-run station. Broadcast from 1971 to 1977, the program featured interviews with guests from the community after which the telephone lines were opened for questions from listeners.

During the 1970s, additional Black faculty were hired, as were Black staff members, particularly in Student Academic Services, the School of Education, and EPHE. According to a special spring 1978 issue of *Invictus* that included photos of sixty-two Black faculty and staff members, "Black teachers, administrators, advisors and civil service workers have had a positive effect in the operation and maintenance of this urban university. Though they have done a good job, they, like students, are a definite minority here at UWM." According to *Invictus*, only 6 percent of the more than 24,000 students attending UWM, and only 3 percent of its 848 faculty were Black. The total number of Black staff members stood at 35.

Meanwhile, in a more promising development, CAAC had become the Department of Afro-American Studies in 1971 and within a few years was offering courses such as The Black Family, The Psychological Effects of Racism, and History of Afro-American Protest. One of its earliest instructors was Ferne Yangyeitie Caulker-Bronson, a native of Sierra Leone who received a bachelor's degree in education from UWM in 1971 and then went on to build the African dance program at its Peck School of the Arts and found Milwaukee's Ko-Thi Dance Company. Caulker-Bronson, today professor emerita in the Department of Dance, recalled the 1960s and 1970s as a time when "race shaped my experience at UWM."

In the 1980s, UWM was establishing itself as a major university. Student services and physical plant facilities finally caught up with student enrollment, and faculty hired in the 1960s and 1970s were establishing themselves as respected scholars in their fields of study. They included Black faculty members widely recognized for their significant contributions to UWM and Milwaukee such as Emma Felder, in nursing, and R. L. McNeely, in social work.

Felder, who held a master's degree from UWM and a PhD from Marquette University, joined the College of Nursing as its first Black professor in 1973.

In 1986, she founded and served as the first director of what today is the Center for Cultural Diversity and Global Health. According to the Wisconsin Historical Society, the center was the "first in the country to facilitate service, research, scholarship, education, and public policy to promote culturally informed, appropriate, competent, and ethical health and well-being in a global context." Felder was a founding member of the Milwaukee chapter of the National Black Nurses Association, a charter member of the Association of Black Nursing Faculty (ABNF), and coeditor of the *ABNF Journal*. She retired in 1996 and was honored in 2003 with an Ernest Spaights Plaza Award.

Professor of Nursing Sandra Millon-Underwood described meeting Felder as a "significant moment" in her own professional development. "Race was a major factor in my experience at the university," said Millon-Underwood, "and I have been afforded exceptional opportunities to work in the community in programs . . . which have given me the opportunity to emulate what I observed in Professor Felder, which was [a commitment] to provide community service."

McNeely, who received his MSW from the University of Michigan and a PhD from Brandeis University, joined the faculty of what was then the School of Social Welfare in 1975, beginning a thirty-seven-year-long career at UWM. Stan Stojkovic, former dean of today's Helen Bader School of Social Welfare, described McNeely—a prolific writer who coauthored an anthology on race and crime in the 1970s and a report on an NAACP study on the status of Black Milwaukeeans in 2011—as "a well-known professor and scholar." Stojkovic told the *Milwaukee Journal Sentinel* that when he met McNeely in 1983, McNeely was a role model "for students who were not used to seeing Black professors on campus. He was one of those initial trailblazers." McNeely, who received a law degree from Marquette University in 1994, worked closely with local social service agencies and cochaired the Felmers O. Chaney Advocacy Board, which advocates for successful reentry into the community for formerly incarcerated individuals.

Virginia G. Stamper, PhD, joined UWM in 1973 as a lecturer in the Department of Afro-American Studies, where for the next thirty years she was renowned for her teaching of Afro-American

▲

*The traditional "hooding" of a doctoral candidate. Left to right: Professor of Educational Psychology Diane M. Pollard, PhD candidate Doris Johnson Browne, and Chancellor Nancy Zimpher.*

literature and composition. According to Vice-Chancellor Emerita Joan M. Prince, Stamper "spoke five languages, was a mentor to many students, and was well respected in the community and professionally."

Another trailblazer hired in the 1970s was Professor of Educational Psychology Diane M. Pollard. A faculty member for more than thirty years, Pollard served as director of the UW System's Center for the Study of Minorities and Disadvantaged from 1979 to 1985. A member of Alpha Kappa Alpha sorority, she was UWM's first recipient of the UW System's Women of Color Award, which she received in 1995. Pollard also received UWM's Distinguished Public Service Award in 1993 and the Spaights Plaza Award in 2009.

Doris Johnson Browne, who began her doctoral work toward a psychology degree at UWM in 1975 and went on to work as counselor and advisor at UWM for more than forty years, knew Pollard as both a professor and colleague. She recalled Pollard stepping in to become her major professor when her initial advisor left UWM. Browne described Pollard as "a wonderful role model for many students no matter what their major was." In an interview, Browne shared her thoughts on her UWM experience, including what she'd learned from Pollard:

> To be Black [here] means to be the best role model that I can. To be willing to advocate no matter how difficult it may

be or no matter what the consequences may be. To do it in such a way that I could feel really good about it and that it will be heard. To really be open and honest about what my concerns are and to put it out there and to be able to talk with people who are in the position to address those areas and a willingness to make the changes.

Following in the footsteps of her mentor, Browne went on to win a 2021 Women of Color Award.

Meanwhile, the Department of Afro-American Studies had begun offering a bachelor's degree in 1980, with students given the choice of concentrating in either political economy and public policy or culture and society. Six years later, students could also pursue a minor in Afro-American studies. Patrick Bellegarde-Smith joined the department in 1986 and served as its chair for three terms before his retirement in 2010. His memories of that time are overwhelmingly positive:

> Upon my arrival to campus, I was in heaven with the number of Black faculty and students on campus. I met on a regular basis on the third floor of the student union to chat with the officers of the Black Student Union [and] that was extremely helpful to me. There was also the Black Faculty Council headed for a very long time by Dean [Mohammed] Aman of [the School of Information

Studies] and . . . that was very helpful as well. The thirty of us [Black faculty members] would meet on a regular basis. . . . We were well established in the community at that point.

No discussion of the 1980s at UWM would be complete without examining the tenure of Clifford V. Smith, the first Black chancellor in the UW System. Smith, who served as chancellor from 1986 to 1990, focused on expanding faculty research, boosting extramural funding, strengthening the rigor of undergraduate education, constructing new facilities, increasing diversity on campus, and improving athletic programs.

Assistant Chancellor for University Relations H. Carl Mueller recalled that although there was excitement among minorities on campus and in the Milwaukee community over Smith's appointment, it was widely recognized that Smith was, indeed, "a chancellor for everyone." In an oral interview recorded in 1990, Smith was asked how being UWM's first Black chancellor had affected the way he operated. "From my perspective, " he responded, "it's had no discernable effect on me whatsoever in terms of doing this job." He noted that the only issues he had encountered with respect to race were related to Black students' misguided expectations that simply because he was Black "things were going to be easier." Smith also said that his tenure should settle the question of "whether or not a minority who had the right background could do the job," adding "I don't think that question should be there anymore."

Smith's contributions to increasing diversity on campus included his Milwaukee Plan, which became part of the UW System's Design for Diversity initiative, a broad effort to recruit minority faculty, staff, and students. According to Smith, who left UWM after four years to become president of the General Electric Foundation, although the Milwaukee Plan worked "reasonably well" for faculty, it was less successful in recruiting staff—due to Civil Service Commission requirements—and students, in part due to the high dropout rate in the Milwaukee Public Schools. Nevertheless, said Smith, "I think that UWM, given the resources that it has, is really running flat out in its external programs to address this problem."

Professor of Economics James Peoples was hired under the Milwaukee Plan, which he described as "an affirmative action mandate to recruit more faculty, staff, students, and administrators of color." The plan, he said, resulted in an increase in the number of Black faculty earning tenure, Black staff receiving indefinite status (equivalent to tenure for faculty members), and Black students enrolling at UWM. Peoples pointed out that two 1993 UWM graduates who were recruited under the Milwaukee Plan went on to work as editors of the only two journals in the country that examine race and economics: Gary Hoover, founder and editor of the *Journal of Economics, Race and Policy,* and Gregory Price, editor of the *Review of Black Political Economy.* Hoover also chaired the economics department at the University of Oklahoma, and in 2021, accepted a position as a professor of economics at Tulane University and director of its Murphy Institute. Noted Peoples, "Prioritizing outreach to minority groups yielded great dividends."

Although UWM had been running pre-college recruitment programs since the late 1960s, such initiatives took on greater urgency in the 1980s. For example, in 1982, Susan Fields, AASAS's program manager, started the first career day exclusively designed for Black students—an event that continues today as UWM's Diversity Career Fair coordinated by the Career Planning and Resource Center and BSCC Program Manager H. Victoria

*Clifford V. Smith, the first Black chancellor in the University of Wisconsin System, initiated the Milwaukee Plan as a way to increase minority faculty, staff, and students.*

▲

April Holland (left), former executive director of UWM's pre-college programs, shares a moment with Shena Harris, a 2016 UWM graduate and former participant in such programs. Photo by Peter Amland.

Pryor. Additionally, Leonard C. White, assistant director of Recruitment & Outreach in the Office of Undergraduate Admissions, encouraged students of color to take part in UWM's U Visit program, which began in 1989. The program has brought hundreds of students—including many of color from cities such as Beloit, Green Bay, Madison, and Kenosha—to campus annually to meet with university faculty and staff about its various academic offerings. Under the leadership of Smith and Assistant Chancellor for Student Affairs C. Scully Stikes, White also created the Multicultural Recognition Program in 1987, a strategy that aimed to recognize Black high school seniors "who were normally not recognized . . . [and present] UWM faculty and staff as caring individuals who wanted them to attend the university." The program attracted approximately three hundred students and five hundred parents from across the state to campus each year. UWM's African American Graduation Celebration, which dates to 1982 and continues today, is designed to take note of the accomplishments of its Black graduates.

Between 1985 and 2000, the Peck School of the Arts sponsored the Community Media Project, which ran media production workshops for youth and teens living in Milwaukee's central city neighborhoods "with the intention of attracting Black students to enroll and become filmmakers." Under the leadership and mentorship of Portia Cobb, who joined the project in 1992, film students assisted with weekend and after-school workshops where they produced documentary videos that were screened at UWM, the Wisconsin Black Historical Society, youth media festivals, and conferences across the nation.

In 1986, UWM began participating in federally funded TRIO Programs, initiatives developed to increase educational opportunities for disadvantaged students in middle and high school, first-generation college students, and individuals with disabilities. Today, UWM offers eight TRIO programs, including Upward Bound and Talent Search. Former Director April Holland recalled "significant moments" associated with the program—noting, in particular, the pride family members of participating students have exhibited.

Efforts to increase diversity on campus were boosted in 1998 when Chancellor Nancy Zimpher announced the creation of the Milwaukee Idea, a groundbreaking initiative embracing community partnerships designed to positively contribute to the university's core research and teaching missions. Following an initial plenary session that drew one hundred participants invited to help develop the initiative—and in response to *UW System Plan 2008: Educational Quality through Racial and Ethnic Diversity*, adopted in 1998—UWM released its own planning document, the *Milwaukee Commitment*. Zimpher tapped Joan M. Prince, at the time an active UWM alum, to work with Gary L. Williams, by then an associate professor of education, to address the document's calls for improvements to the "social, working, and learning aspects of campus life for people of all cultures."

In 2000, the African American Academic Staff Council, created in 1993 to increase the number of Black staff on campus, merged with the Black Faculty Council, organized in 1980 and described as a "primary social and networking outlet for Black faculty and staff," to form the African American Faculty & Staff Council. Staff members Kathy Berry and Brenda Cullin were instrumental in leading the council, which ran blood and school supply drives, awarded scholarships to Black UWM students, and recognized Black faculty and staff for their accomplishments and achievements.

That same year, Zimpher appointed Prince vice-chancellor for partnerships and innovation, formalizing her responsibility for implementing the Milwaukee Commitment. And in spring 2001, the Wisconsin State Legislature approved more than $16 million in new funding to implement the Milwaukee Idea. Today vice-chancellor emerita, Prince recalls the move as "the first time that the legislature allocated funds to a UW System campus with the specific purpose of improving diversity and community partnerships."

In November 2002, at the request of the African American Faculty & Staff Council—today the African Diaspora Council—Zimpher charged Prince and Larry G. Martin, chair of the School of Education's Department of Administrative Leadership, with organizing and leading the university's Task Force on Race and Ethnicity, designed to assess the state of diversity at UWM and develop recommendations for creating an organizational culture that reflected the diversity of university employees. The task force's findings, updated with focus group and climate survey data, determined "the campus climate falls short of being one that accepts and accommodates people of color," and noted a "lack of skill and training at all levels in diversity issues and in managing interpersonal conflicts, the lack of critical mass of diverse faculty, staff and students in many units, and inadequate mentoring and advancement opportunities. . . . " Martin, today professor emeritus, was a 2021 recipient of an Ernest Spaights Plaza Award.

Yet another initiative designed to address the lack of diversity on campus was the Diversity Fellows program, which ran between 2009 and 2012, and gave underrepresented students with terminal degrees and PhD candidates the chance to gain teaching experience or pursue research. In some cases, fellows were invited to apply for tenure-track positions at UWM. The program, under the leadership of Interim Associate Vice-Chancellor for Diversity and Climate Cheryl Ajirotutu, was also a means for UWM to strengthen its academic program.

Meanwhile, in 1994, the Department of

Professor of Africology Winston Van Horne, who came to UWM in 1978, was instrumental in shaping the Department of Africology (now the Department of African and African Diaspora Studies).

Afro-American Studies had been renamed the Department of Africology. (According to university records, the term "Africology" was coined by Winston Van Horne, longtime department chair, "to reflect the focus on experiences of people of African descent all over the world.") In 2010, the department welcomed its first doctoral students, and two years later, its first master's students. In 2018, it changed its name to the Department of African and African Diaspora Studies, "to signify a global focus [that also] reflects changing norms and attitudes about nomenclature within the discipline." Courses examine "issues facing people of African descent all over the world, including in sub-Saharan Africa, Latin America, the Caribbean, Europe, and the United States." According to Associate Professor Anika Wilson, one of the most popular instructors in the department was the late Ahmed Mbalia, senior lecturer emeritus, who over twenty-three years taught hundreds of students and was well known for his strong connections to the Milwaukee community.

Unfortunately, despite decades of recruitment efforts targeting Black students and faculty, the development of scores of initiatives aimed at supporting Black students, and the growth of African and African Diaspora studies, the number of African Americans on campus remains regrettably low. Cullin, recipient of the 2021 University Staff Excellence Award, worked at UWM for forty-two years before retiring at the end of 2021 as office manager in the Department of Economics. She

Senior Lecturer Emeritus Ahmed Mbalia, who spent twenty-three years at UWM, was among the most popular instructors in the Department of Africology. Photo courtesy Wisconsin Bail Out the People Movement.

# NUMBER AND PERCENTAGE OF BLACK FACULTY, STAFF, AND STUDENTS

| CATEGORY | 1997 | 2007 | 2017 | 2020 |
|---|---|---|---|---|
| **BLACK STAFF AND FACUTLY** | **483 or 14.1%** of all employees<br><br>N = 3,420 | **419 or 11%** of all employees<br><br>N = 3,806 | **388 or 10%** of all employees<br><br>N = 3,880 | **333 or 8.6%** of all employees<br><br>N = 3,864 |
| **BLACK FACULTY ONLY** | **27 or 4%** of all tenured and non-tenured faculty<br><br>N = 670 | **46 or 5.9%** of all tenured and non-tenured faculty<br><br>N = 770 | **33 or 4.5%** of all tenured and non-tenured faculty<br><br>N = 729 | **29 or 4%** of all tenured and non-tenured faculty<br><br>N = 732 |
| **BLACK STUDENTS** | **1,852 or 8.3%** of all UWM students<br><br>N = 22,251 | **1,913 or 6.5%** of all UWM students<br><br>N = 29,358 | **1,796 or 7%** of all UWM students<br><br>N = 25,412 | **1,507 or 6.5%** of all UWM students<br><br>N = 23,004 |

*N = Total number of all employees, tenured and non-tenured faculty, and students of all races*
*Sources: UWM Department of Human Resources and UWM Office of Assessment and Institutional Research*

noted that "the Black [university] community has dwindled substantially . . . from the faculty all the way down to the students."

The disheartening statistics, summarized in the table above, bear Cullin out. Consider, for example, that the overall number of Black faculty and staff decreased by 31 percent between 1997—when the figure stood at 483, or 14 percent of all faculty and staff—to just 333, or 8.6 percent of the total, in 2020, according to UWM's Office of Institutional Research. Over the same period, the number and percentage of Black faculty members remained relatively stable. As for Black students, enrollment between 1997 and 2020 dropped 18.6 percent, in part due to the enrollment decreases campus wide.

If such data are disappointing, comfort can be taken from the impact that programs and initiatives initially designed to support Black students, staff, and faculty have had on other students on campus. Williams credits Spaights with laying the groundwork for that impact, noting, "He knew that many students were coming to UWM underprepared and he gave UWM the capacity to serve all students underprepared for

post-secondary education. . . ." One such example is the broad impact of EPHE, which has operated in the past as both the Academic Opportunity Center and the Office of Central Advising and is today UWM's Pathway Advising program. It is described by the university as "as a temporary home for new freshman students who are undecided about their college major or who are determined through the admission process to need additional support before transitioning into their chosen major." Pathway advisors work intensely with students, regularly monitoring their progress and ensuring they receive opportunities to "build their academic skills" and "make informed decisions about their major and/or future career."

*Brenda Cullin's forty-two-year-long career at UWM was honored with a University Staff Excellence Award from the University of Wisconsin Board of Regents in 2021. Photo by Troye Fox.*

*Phillip A. Clark, first Black chief of police, UWM Police Department.*

*James Hill, UWM's first Black dean of students.* Photo courtesy James Hill.

*Arcetta S. Knautz, the first Black director of UWM University Housing.*

As we come to the end of this story, here are a few more significant contributions Black faculty, staff, and alumni have made, and continue to make, both to UWM and the greater Milwaukee community:

○ — Joan M. Prince served as a UWM vice-chancellor from 2000 until her retirement in 2021, designing and implementing campus-wide and global initiatives such as the STEM-Inspire Program, the Inclusive Internationalization Project, Global Partnerships in STEM, and the Center for International Health—all aimed at increasing the number of faculty and students from underrepresented groups. In 2012, she was named Alternate Representative to the 67th session of the General Assembly of the United Nations by President Barack Obama, holding the honorary rank of ambassador.

○ — Mohammed Aman served from 1979 to 2002 as the second dean of what today is the School of Information Studies (SOIS). Aman, who retired in 2020, was also founder of the UWM Black Faculty Council. He retired in 2020.

○ — Phillip A. Clark served from 1990 to 2004 as the first Black chief of police for the UWM Police Department. Prior to that, he was the first Black Wisconsin state trooper, and the first to achieve the rank of lieutenant. Clark was an Ernest Spaights Plaza Awardee in 2016.

○ — James Hill served as associate vice-chancellor and interim senior student affairs officer. He was also UWM's first Black dean of students, holding that post from 1996 to 1998 (interim), 1998 to 2006, 2007 to 2009, and 2010 to 2011.

○ — Richard Cox, who received his bachelor's degree in criminal justice in 1974, was the first Black president of the UWM Alumni Association, serving from 1999 to 2001; a recipient of the university's Distinguished Alumni Award in 2001; and a member of UWM's 1970s All-Decade basketball team. Cox also made his mark on Milwaukee, as a member of the Milwaukee Fire and Police Commission from 2005 to 2013; superintendent of the Milwaukee County House of Corrections from 1993 to 2001; and executive director of Neighborhood House, a community center focused on meeting the needs of families and children in the city's underserved areas, from 2008 to 2014.

○ — Arcetta S. Knautz was named director of UWM University Housing in 2018, the first Black female in the state of Wisconsin to hold such a position. Knautz not only managed a budget of approximately $26 million and 300 employees, but also oversaw approximately 4,300 students residing on campus and 300 employees.

○ — Stanley Battle held the Sullivan-Spaights Professorship—at the time, the only professorship named after an African American in the entire UW System—from 1998 to 2001. He worked in the School of Education and what was then the School of Social Welfare.

- — David J. Pate Jr., associate professor in the Helen Bader School of Social Welfare, chair of the school's Department of Social Work, and an expert on low-income African American men, fatherhood, and child support, was named the recipient of the Spaights Endowment, a grant that supports research on poverty, in 2009. Pate also received UWM's Faculty Distinguished Undergraduate Teacher Award in 2018 and was named a member of the university's 2021–2022 Global Fellows team charged with developing a course on the Black Lives Matter movement.

- — Chukuka S. Enwemeka served as the first Black dean of the College of Health Sciences from 2009 to 2014 and was awarded Distinguished Professor status in 2012. He is the foremost authority on photo engineering of the tissue repair process with visible and near infrared light and lasers.

- — Anthony Ross was the inaugural holder of the Rockwell Automation Endowed Chair in Supply Chain Management, established in the Sheldon B. Lubar School of Business in 2010. During his tenure at UWM, Ross oversaw the design and launch of a new supply chain curriculum that quickly became the largest program of its kind in the state.

Kelby Spann (center), the first Black man to hold the position of director of an office of student services, with staff members Kate Masshardt (left) and Talisa M. Smith (right), 2018.

- — Deryl Davis Fulmer, in the School of Education, and Kelby Spann, in the Helen Bader School of Social Welfare, were the first— and to date, only—Black staff at UWM to oversee offices of student services.

- — Kent Wilburn has worked in environmental services at UWM for forty-five years, beginning in 1977. He is one of the university's longest-serving employees.

- — In 2010, Wilkistar Otieno became the first Black female faculty member hired in the College of Engineering & Applied Science and, in 2018, the first Black woman to chair the Industrial and Manufacturing Engineering Department. Her successful collaboration with Rockwell Automation contributed to the establishment of the Connected Systems Institute at UWM.

- — Elizabeth Drame, professor in the School of Education, and Gladys Mitchell-Walthour, associate professor in the Department of African and African Diaspora Studies, were recipients of Fulbright grants in 2011 and 2020, respectively.

In 2010, Wilkistar Otieno became the first Black female faculty member hired in the College of Engineering & Applied Science.

In conclusion, the documented journey of Black folk and their effect on the formation of institutions has often relied on the oral histories of those who have experienced such developments. The voices of the esteemed contributors chronicled in this chapter have provided solid evidence of their successes, challenges, and ongoing contributions with respect to the creation of UWM.

CHAPTER

# 3

# Demanding a Place at the Table: Latino Militancy and Contributions at UWM

Joseph A. Rodríguez and
William Vélez

*Staff and students from the Roberto Hernández Center at the University of Wisconsin-Milwaukee (UWM) at the city's Mexican Fiesta, 2019. Back row, left: Colin Flanner. Front row, left to right: Michael Vazquez, Briceida Janely Perez, Pounce the Panther, Rebecca Arcos-Piedra, and Violeta Ramirez. Back row, right: Gabriela Dorantes.*

The roots of Latinx education at the University of Wisconsin-Milwaukee (UWM) can be traced to the efforts of local activists who as early as 1968 began calling out the University of Wisconsin System's failure to address the needs of the Latino community. Over the next fifty years, they and their successors would fight for programs and initiatives designed not only to recruit, retain, and support Latinx students, faculty, and staff, but also to celebrate their accomplishments. The early 2000s would see the appointment of the university's first Latino chancellor, a point of pride for the Latino community. And today, with UWM enrolling about a quarter of all Latinx students in the UW System, the school is taking steps to qualify as a federally designated Hispanic Serving Institution.

This chapter, which includes material previously published online in Joseph A. Rodríguez's paper "Latinos at UWM: A History of the Spanish Speaking Outreach Institute," uses the ethnic terms Hispanic, Latino/Latina, and Latinx. Hispanic is a US government term that replaced older terms such as Spanish American and Latin. The term Hispanic declined in popularity in the 1990s as the Latino community embraced Spanish-language terminology such as Latino/Latina. However, Latinx has grown in popularity in the last ten years because it avoids gender specificity and includes individuals who identify as nonbinary. We use the term Hispanic when we review statistics collected under that category.

In 1950 there were about 12,500 Latinos in Milwaukee, including approximately 10,000 Mexicans and 2,500 Puerto Ricans. By 1970, Milwaukee's Latino population had increased to around 30,000. Several factors explain the increase: Immigration from Mexico and migration from south Texas to the Midwest continued, and although Mexicans still made up most of the agricultural workforce, mechanization of agriculture drove more rural migrants to move into the cities. Labor contractors working for Milwaukee factory owners, assisted by Puerto Rican Department of Labor officials in Chicago, worked with employers to entice workers to the city and its factories. Finally, some Latinos came to the area to attend college.

In the 1960s and 1970s, campuses throughout the US were rife not only with anti–Vietnam War protests, but also civil rights activism that resulted in the creation of African American Studies programs. The first Mexican American Studies program was created at Cal State Los Angeles in 1968. That same year, protests by Black and Puerto Rican students at City College of New York, part of the City University of New York (CUNY) system, led in 1970 to the first Puerto Rican Studies program (today Puerto Rican and Latino Studies) at CUNY's Brooklyn College.

Milwaukee in 1967 and 1968 saw the city's African Americans—along with Father James Groppi, Catholic priest and community activist, and Vel Phillips, the first Black woman to win a seat on the Milwaukee City Council—march from the city's North Side to the South Side for nearly two hundred consecutive days to bring awareness of the discriminatory housing policies the city continued to uphold. In 1968, Groppi rallied Milwaukee Latinos to protest what was then the Allen-Bradley Company, a manufacturer of factory automation equipment, demanding more Latino employment at the company. Mexican American and Puerto Rican activists also assumed control of nonprofit organizations such as the United Migrant Opportunity Services (UMOS) that —although

mostly serving Latino migrant workers—was led by non-Latinos.

That same year, Latino activists in Milwaukee formed the Latin American Union for Civil Rights (LAUCR), whose founders and leaders included Ernesto Chacon, Roberto Hernández, Avelardo Valdez, and Juan Alvarez Cuauhtémoc. The group created the community newspaper *La Guardia* and protested police brutality and housing and job discrimination. Soon, however, these concerns gave way to a focus on education, and particularly the expansion of bilingual education opportunities.

Such efforts had begun in 1967, when Ernest Spaights, a UWM professor of education, created the Experimental Program in Higher Education to boost admission of minority and disadvantaged students who, despite their potential, would not otherwise have gained entry to the university. In 1968, Father John Maurice of Milwaukee, one of the founders of the nonprofit Spanish Center on the city's South Side, wrote a letter to University of Wisconsin Extension Division Chancellor Henry Ahlgren criticizing the UW System's lack of efforts to serve the Latino community. This led to a series of community meetings between Extension Division leaders, social service agency officials, and Latinx community activists. These discussions stressed the need for GED and English as a Second Language (ESL) classes, and increased attention

*Latinx students march on the office of UWM Chancellor J. Martin Klotsche on August 26, 1970.*

to Latinx student recruitment. In 1969, Education Professor Salomón Hernández Flores helped create the High School Equivalency Program to assist students who had dropped out of high school earn their GEDs and gain admission to college. The School of Education also launched programs in bilingual education teacher training secured with government funding. Despite these new programs, Latinx activists felt the university should do more for the Latinx community.

In 1969, the Council for the Education of Latin Americans (CELA) was formed, growing out of LAUCR. Richard Davis, dean of the School of Education, agreed to work with CELA on developing education programs in the Latino community and improving Latino access to UWM. He also gave community members a central role in the formation and management of programs designed to improve conditions for Latinos at UWM.

Yet, UWM administrators—including Chancellor J. Martin Klotsche—offered little support for establishing new programs specifically for Latinos. As a result, protestors demonstrated outside Chapman Hall on August 26, 1970.

▲

*Protestors stage a sit-in at Klotsche's office, demanding that UWM increase the number of Latinx students, faculty, and staff on campus.*

The next day, CELA was scheduled to meet with Klotsche, but the chancellor failed to attend the meeting. CELA members and about one hundred other Latino activists, mostly non-students, then staged a day-long sit-in at the chancellor's office. Most had left by five thirty that evening, but five protestors were arrested: Marla O. Anderson, Dante Navarro, Gregorio J. (Goyo) Rivera, Jesus Salas, and José Luis Huerta-Sánchez. Others active in the movement included Ernesto Chacon, Roberto Hernández, Clementina Castro, Enriqueta González, María Ortega, Juanita Rentería, Rev. Jaime Davila, Luis López, Dagoberto Ibarra, and Delfina Guzmán.

In response, Hernández, a leader of LAUCR and CELA, wrote a letter to the University of Wisconsin Board of Regents critical of Klotsche and other UWM administrators. He and other Latino activists demanded that UWM create a new institute to serve Latino students.

Instead, the administration proposed expanding already existing programs and sending four recruiters into the Latino community. In September 1970, CELA consulted with lawyers about filing a lawsuit against the university for the misappropriation of federal funds designated for minority programming and Klotsche and CELA entered into negotiations. CELA clarified what it wanted: a permanent institute with offices located both inside the chancellor's office and on the city's South Side. CELA also set a recruitment goal of eighty-five new Latino admits, comprised of ten graduate students, fifty undergraduates, and twenty-five recent high school graduates and special students. CELA also demanded that

◀ *Roberto Hernández was an early Latino activist at UWM.*

*A drum circle outside of Mitchell Hall during the demonstrations leading to the establishment of the Spanish Speaking Outreach Institute at UWM, August 1970.*

students receive college credit for work in the community and that UWM create a GED program, scholarships, and grants for Latinx students.

Protesters returned to UWM in October, and despite the chilly weather, slept on the grass in front of the chancellor's office for several nights. There ensued a series of additional protests, including a hunger strike on campus and a march up North Lake Drive by students and community members who picketed outside Chancellor Klotsche's home. With negotiations stalled, CELA led a delegation to a University of Wisconsin Board of Regents meeting in Madison, criticizing UWM administration for inaction. After the meeting, UWM administration approved the creation of the Spanish Speaking Outreach Institute (SSOI), a move announced by CELA and Klotsche on October 23, 1970.

SSOI was in operation by November 1, 1970, with an office on campus in a house at 3261 N. Maryland Ave. and a site on the city's South Side at 805 S. Fifth St. in a building that also housed *La Guardia*. Ricardo Fernández, who had been involved in the negotiations resulting in the creation of SSOI, had left his position as a professor at Marquette University to become a special assistant to the chancellor and SSOI's first director. His staff included Assistant Director Armando Orellana, administrative assistant Celia Pérez, and two ESL teachers.

The South Side office of SSOI offered classes in ESL and social work, academic and financial aid advising, training for day care workers, and community organizing. Under Fernández's

direction, SSOI staff also offered a GED program, advised and advocated for Latinx students, directed the recruitment and retention of students and staff, and provided outreach into the Milwaukee Latinx community. Fernández pushed UWM to hire Latinx faculty and to offer courses in Caribbean and Mexican American studies. (He would later create a course on Hispanics in education.) The results of these efforts were impressive: in fall 1971, UWM enrolled 150 Latinx students, a number that would jump to 351 by fall 1975. Furthermore, a 1972 CELA evaluation report on the institute's work noted that in the fall of 1971 a total of 210 students had utilized SSOI services. They included 140 students who had not met UWM's regular admission requirements and would not have been admitted without some special consideration or support.

On July 1, 1973, SSOI moved into the College of Letters and Science to allow it to develop course offerings. However, even before the transfer, some Letters and Science faculty had been critical of SSOI. John H. Schroeder, professor of history emeritus, spent his entire career at UWM, and served as its fifth chancellor from 1990 to 1998. He recalled, in a recent interview, that the criticism stemmed from "academic differences" between those who took a "traditional approach to teaching Spanish language and literature and those advocating for the newly emerging Hispanic studies." Indeed, such criticism would turn out to foreshadow the institute's future problems. Fernández resigned after less than one year at the helm of SSOI to go to law school but returned in spring 1972 to become an assistant to the dean in the School of Education and serve in an advising capacity with the institute. In 1988, he would assume the position of assistant vice-chancellor for academic affairs, also serving as coordinator of the Division of Academic Affairs' newly established M/D (Multicultural/Disadvantaged) Office.

In the 1970s and 1980s, SSOI had a series of directors who were also faculty in the Department of Spanish and Portuguese. They included Arnoldo C. Vento (Mexican American), Rodolfo J. Cortina (Cuban), and Santiago Daydi-Tolson (Chilean). In 1976, Felipe Rodríguez (Puerto Rican) completed his undergraduate degree at the University of Illinois and came to UWM as an advisor to SSOI under Vento. (At that time, SSOI had two Mexican American advisors and a Mexican American director; as a result, there was community pressure to hire a Puerto Rican.)

Vento reoriented SSOI by concentrating on the arts—and particularly literature classes—and led SSOI to cosponsor a cultural event, Canto el Pueblo. Research also became a significant part of the mission of SSOI, and in the 1970s and 1980s the institute published a series of papers on topics such as the literary work and sociological experiences of Latino Milwaukee. Cortina, for example, coedited with Frederico Herrera the publication of a facsimile edition of a historic newsletter, *El Mutualista*, originally published in Milwaukee from 1947 to 1950. Other SSOI publications included the results of a study on the Puerto Rican family and migration written by UWM School of Social Welfare professor José B. Torres and a directory of Latino agencies in Wisconsin compiled by Arnoldo Sevilla and edited by Elly Seng. Additional SSOI-sponsored research studies were written by Joan Moore, Anna Akulicz Santiago, and William Vélez.

By 1980, there were 383 Latino undergraduate students at UWM. Student groups on campus included La Colectiva and Movimiento Estudiantil Chicano De Aztlán. Undergraduate Ruben Burgos (who went on to become a police officer and detective in the Milwaukee Police Department) was president of La Colectiva in 1985–1986. These Latinx student groups became an important source of support for SSOI; when administrators threatened budget cuts, SSOI directors could call on their members to lobby administration officials. (Directors also routinely called on Latino community leaders and faculty supporters to pen letters supporting the maintenance of funding for SSOI.)

Yet signs of potential problems for SSOI had surfaced as early as 1979, when under William Halloran, dean of the College of Letters and Science, SSOI's South Side offices were closed. (By then Cortina, who had taught for SSOI and served as director of Latin American Studies at UWM, had succeeded Vento as institute director, a post he would hold until 1983.) What's more, by the mid-1980s, Latinx campus and community members were seriously questioning UWM's commitment to SSOI. As it turned out, their concerns were merited. Indeed, in 1987, Halloran moved SSOI—its budget reduced and its advising role assumed by a new advising group, Hispanic Student Academic Services—out of the College of Letters and Science, and into the Division of Student Affairs. Felipe Rodríguez, who had earned a master's degree in education in 1988, assumed the position of SSOI director after Santiago Daydi-Tolson left the directorship in 1989.

Rodríguez concluded, in his master's thesis, that the changes represented a "shift away from outreach and community involvement activity to a focus on student retention through increased advising and accessing of support services from other UWM support service units." Latinos on and off campus criticized the changes and viewed the fragmentation of services as detrimental. However, despite these changes to SSOI, the Latino student population continued to grow, reaching 749 by 1995. Course choices expanded as well, with students now able to take Latino-centric courses in the departments of history, English, Spanish and Portuguese, sociology, political science, and education. Other courses would eventually appear in the departments of theater, film, and architecture.

By the early 1990s, SSOI had become a shell of its former self and there was little Latino activism on campus. That would change in 1992, when Robert Miranda—an ex-marine and and assistant prison warden—arrived on campus. Miranda, born in Chicago but of Puerto Rican descent, had moved to Milwaukee after his wife was named a US marshal here. On campus, he met and befriended another undergraduate, Bernardino "Nino" Alvarez, a fellow military veteran. One day while Alvarez was working in the Golda Meir Library, a staff member told him to leave, calling him a "vagabond." After Alvarez told Miranda of the incident, they returned to the library and confronted the staff member, resulting in a call to UWM police. Miranda and Alvarez then went to the only Latino student group on campus, the Hispanic Student Association

*Enrique Figueroa (front row, center), director of the Roberto Hernández Center from 2002 to 2016, with graduates of the Latino Nonprofit Leadership Program.*

(HSA), to seek support but discovered that the HSA was primarily a social group and not interested in getting involved. In response, Alvarez and Miranda formed the Latin Student Union (LSU), which became an official student group in January 1993. The group's core members included Elba Torres, Miguel Soto, Bobbi Lipeles, and Marshall Vega.

Researching SSOI's history, Miranda and Alvarez came to understand the negative impact of the institute's split from the College of Letters and Science in 1987. Miranda concluded that the university had misappropriated funds designated by the UW System for minority programming and confronted UWM officials with his evidence. (Notably, Ricardo Fernández, SSOI's first director, had found similar discrepancies around the use of SSOI funds by Letters and Science administrators years earlier.) What's more, both campus and community Latinx activists could see that SSOI was stagnating, and LSU began pressuring the university, and specifically Marshall Goodman, dean of the College of Letters and Science, to reinvigorate SSOI. In the early 1990s, Goodman proved to be receptive, bringing the institute and Rodríguez back into the college. LSU also advocated for the creation of the Latino Studies Certificate Program (LSCP), which launched in 1994.

In 1995, Latinx students, faculty, staff, and community members proposed the creation of a new center that would not only replace SSOI, but also incorporate LSCP and all Latinx advising services. The new center, created one year later, was named the Roberto Hernández Center (RHC) to honor one of the original leaders of the SSOI movement. Vélez, professor of sociology, was named interim director, with Felipe Rodríguez

continuing to serve as head recruiter. After a national search, Manuel Martín-Rodríguez was hired as an associate professor in the Department of Spanish and Portuguese and RHC director, a position he held through 2000. In addition, two new recruiters were hired.

Meanwhile, Latinos on and off campus remained convinced that the RHC should serve all UWM's Latino students, not just those in Letters and Science, because more Latinx students were majoring in education, engineering, nursing, social welfare, and business. In 2000, the Chancellor's Latino/Hispanic Advisory Committee recommended that RHC be housed in the provost's office to afford students in all the colleges better access to RHC's services.

In 2002, following a national search, Enrique Figueroa was named director of the RHC. Figueroa—a native Texan with a doctorate in agricultural economics from the University of California, Davis—had worked in the US Department of Agriculture under President Bill Clinton and as a faculty member at Cornell University before coming to UWM as an assistant professor. While RHC director, Figueroa received funds from the Hispanics in Philanthropy Funders' Collaborative for Strong Latino Communities to launch the Latino Nonprofit Leadership Program in 2005. This eleven-month-long program graduated nearly two hundred students, including the current RHC director, Alberto J. Maldonado, and former State Representative JoCasta Zamarripa. Other graduates included Angela Fernandez, who later earned a doctorate in social work from the University of Washington in Seattle; Marcela "Xela" Garcia, currently executive director of the Walker's Point Center for the Arts and a Milwaukee Public School Board member; Bernabe Gonzalez, former executive director and current president of the board of directors of Stewards of Prophetic, Hopeful, International Action, a faith-based nonprofit in Waukesha, Wisconsin; Melissa Flores, who earned a master's degree from Harvard University's Graduate School of Education, and a doctorate in Chicano Studies from the University of California, Santa Barbara; and Rebeca M. López, who went on to earn earned her law degree at Marquette University.

Figueroa also founded Promoting Academics in Latino Milwaukee (PALM), an annual fundraiser celebrating UWM's Latinx graduates. (The event's proceeds fund scholarships for UWM Latinx students.) He also created the Outstanding Community Member Award given to notable Latino leaders annually. Figueroa served in the UWM Faculty Senate, on the University Committee, and on the boards of directors of numerous community organizations (e.g., UMOS, Council for the Spanish Speaking, Planned Parenthood, Big Brothers/ Big Sisters, and the Milwaukee Public Market). He moderated the Milwaukee PBS television show *4th Street Forum* and brought to campus many distinguished speakers. In 2008, Figueroa was named the recipient of the Congressional Hispanic Caucus Institute's Distinguished Alumnus Award.

In July 2004, Carlos E. Santiago became the seventh chancellor of the University of Wisconsin-Milwaukee. Santiago had been born in Puerto Rico and, as the son of a US Army career veteran who had fought in World War II, Korea, and Vietnam, traveled throughout the world. Santiago met his wife, Azara Lourdes Rivera, while in high school when both their fathers were stationed at Fort Buchanan, Puerto Rico. Both Santiago and Rivera went on to earn their doctorate degrees while starting a family. Upon her husband's appointment as chancellor, Rivera-Santiago joined the UWM faculty as an associate professor in the School of Education's Department of Educational Psychology.

Ricardo Diaz, at the time executive director of Milwaukee's United Community Center (UCC), was a member of the search committee that recommended Santiago's

▲

*Carlos E. Santiago became UWM's seventh chancellor—and its first Latinx chancellor—in 2004. During his tenure, Santiago significantly increased UWM's public and private funding, raised its academic profile, and spearheaded the creation of the School of Freshwater Sciences and the Joseph J. Zilber School of Public Health.* Photo courtesy Carlos E. Santiago.

appointment as chancellor. "First and foremost, from the committee's perspective, it was Carlos's experience—particularly his economic development background—that made him such an attractive candidate," recalled Diaz in a recent interview. "But the fact that he was Hispanic certainly was a plus and a point of pride for the Latino community," which he said was "absolutely thrilled" with Santiago's appointment.

Indeed, in selecting Santiago as chancellor, the UW Regents and President Katharine Lyall most importantly chose a leader who would strengthen UWM's national academic reputation and increase its chances of becoming a major research university. In his plenary address to faculty, staff, and students in September 2004, Santiago expressed his belief that UWM needed to raise its academic profile, stating that the key to achieving this aspirational goal "will lie in our ability to expand and diversify our sources of funding to the campus, primarily through the expansion of extramural support for our research, and donated or philanthropic funds." He then proposed the creation of two new doctoral programs each year until the total number offered reached thirty.

*Chancellor Carlos E. Santiago (far right) and a UWM delegation tour Puerto Rican universities and recruit students to UWM. Left to right: Azara Rivera-Santiago, Sheldon Lubar, Marianne Lubar, Lisa Cudahy, Michael Cudahy, Margarita Benitez, Mary Kellner, and Ted Kellner.*
Photo courtesy Carlos E. Santiago.

Under Santiago, the UWM Foundation created the UWM Real Estate Foundation and charged it with initiating and funding—through the issuance of tax-exempt bonds—construction projects such as new student dormitories. The foundation, under the leadership of David Gilbert, who had initially served as Santiago's assistant, opened the Kenilworth Square Apartments between North Farwell and North Prospect avenues in 2006, and two years later, the RiverView Hall student residence at 2340 N. Commerce St. These facilities offered space for nearly 450 students.

Chancellor Santiago set a goal of raising research expenditures at UWM to $100 million; to attain that goal he launched a program that would provide seed funds for those faculty research projects most likely to become self-sustaining over the long term or lead to entrepreneurial endeavors. His Research Growth Initiative (RGI) ultimately provided faculty with $3.5 million in grants to develop new research proposals and secure funds from outside sources.

Santiago directed that most of RGI's attention be devoted to expanding research in the sciences, technology, engineering, and mathematics. By 2008, he had secured $10 million in state funds used to bring on additional faculty, including twenty-two new hires in the College of Engineering & Applied Science. (Santiago also worked with the UWM Foundation on its 2006 Campaign for UWM, which raised a record-setting $125 million for the university.)

Santiago's efforts to expand UWM's academic offerings were rewarded in 2008, when the UW Board of Regents approved two new schools: the School of Freshwater Sciences and the School of

Public Health, named for Joseph J. Zilber, the late philanthropist and early champion of the school who pledged $10 million toward its creation. In 2017, the Joseph J. Zilber School of Public Health, which operates out of the former Pabst Brewery complex in downtown Milwaukee, became the first nationally accredited school of public health in Wisconsin. The School of Freshwater Sciences had its origins in the Great Lakes Water Institute, a freshwater research institution of the UW System administered by UWM's Graduate School. In the early 2000s, the school was housed in an aging building in Milwaukee's inner harbor. With the help of state funds, a new $53 million facility opened in fall 2014 at 600 E. Greenfield Ave.

Over the course of his tenure as chancellor, Santiago helped UWM increase its enrollment by 12 percent, the number of doctoral degrees available by 87 percent, and total research funding by 89 percent. These accomplishments, and in particular the increase in the number of graduate degrees earned by its students, proved to be crucial reasons why in 2016—six years after Santiago's departure—UWM would be named a Level I research university by the Carnegie Classification of Institutions of Higher Education.

According to Diaz, who retired from the UCC in 2020, Santiago established strong, close connections to Latino Milwaukee. "All in all, he became an incredible asset, not only because of the skills he brought, but also because his presence at many local activities gave a lift to the community and many of its issues were heightened by his presence," he said. Diaz also recalled Rivera-Santiago's significant contributions in the area of mental health, noting, "They were quite a team and packed an incredible one-two punch." Diaz also sees Santiago's appointment as a move that went a long way toward highlighting UWM's commitment to racial diversity. "At the time, the university was already heading down that path," Diaz recalled. "But having someone at the very top absolutely advanced that mission."

Following Wisconsin Governor Scott Walker's election in 2010, the university was hit with sharp budget cuts and a tuition freeze, and although Latinx issues were beginning to command more attention, the RHC budget was reduced. Furthermore, UWM's track record with respect to the growth in Hispanic faculty would fluctuate over the next ten years. Consider, for example, that full-time Hispanic faculty numbered fifteen in 1997 and rose to forty-three in 2010 before declining to thirty-five in 2020. (Permanent Hispanic staff increased from nineteen in 1997 to forty-five in 2020.)

Yet UWM Hispanic faculty members were gaining wide recognition, particularly in the arts. Professor of English Mauricio Kilwein Guevara, a featured speaker at national poetry conferences, served as a curator at what is now Milwaukee's Woodland Pattern Book Center, and Associate Professor of English Brenda Cárdenas was named Milwaukee's 2010–2012 poet laureate. Professor of Music René Izquierdo, an internationally renowned classical guitarist originally from Cuba who has performed as a solo recitalist, chamber musician, and soloist with orchestras worldwide, founded the UWM guitar program in 2004, leading it to national prominence. And Associate Professor of Playwriting Alvaro Saar Rios, who joined UWM in 2010, co-founded The Royal Mexican Players, a national touring performance troupe, and created work for theatrical organizations such as the Houston Grand Opera and the Honolulu Theater for Youth. In 2019, Rios was named a playwright-in-residence at First Stage, Milwaukee's children's theater.

Notable among UWM's administrative ranks was Professor of Mechanical Engineering Ronald A. Perez, who also served as chair of that department and as dean of the College of Engineering & Applied Science. In 2018, Perez—who hailed from the Dominican Republic—was appointed dean of the Joseph J. Zilber School of Public Health, playing an important role in the new school's creation and accreditation. He also cochaired the committee that oversaw the unification of the UW System's Milwaukee, Waukesha, and Washington County campuses.

Meanwhile, despite its budget woes, RHC in 2010 had helped create what is now UWM's Latin American, Caribbean, & U.S. Latinx Studies (LACUSL) interdisciplinary major, providing

*Associate Professor of English Brenda Cárdenas teaches creative writing and US Latinx literature, is an established author, and served as Milwaukee Poet Laureate from 2010 to 2012. A recorded reading of her work is included in the Library of Congress's "Spotlight on U. S. Hispanic Writers."* Photo courtesy Brenda Cárdenas.

*Professor of Music René Izquierdo (right), an internationally renowned classical guitar virtuoso, instructs senior UWM student Leonela Alejandro, a promising young guitarist and winner of several international guitar competitions.* Photo courtesy René Izquierdo.

*Associate Professor Alvaro Saar Rios advising UWM Theatre students, 2016.* Photo by Joe Mazza.

students with a curriculum that integrates study of the Latin American region with that of Latinx people within the United States. During the 2019–2020 school year, there were ten students pursuing the LACUSL major. What's more, RHC's retention programs have increased the six-year Latinx graduation rate from 29.4 percent in 2010 to 36.2 percent in 2020. Unfortunately, it still trails that of white students, which in 2020 stood at 47.6 percent.

Alberto J. Maldonado succeeded Figueroa as interim director of RHC in 2016, becoming permanent director two years later. Maldonado had served as a student worker in SSOI while earning his bachelor's degree in fine arts at UWM in 1996. He then earned a master's degree in education policy in 2010 and worked as an advisor in UWM's pre-college programs and as the university's assistant director for recruitment. Maldonado revived the PALM event by combining it with RHC graduation ceremonies; as the center's endowment grew, he also increased the number of emergency scholarships awarded annually. He spearheaded the production of UWM's first bilingual viewbook and was involved as well in intentional branding and marketing to the Latinx community. Under Maldonado's leadership, UWM continued Casa Abierta, a bilingual open house for new admits, increased UWM's presence at local high school and community events, and stepped up its recruitment and outreach efforts.

In 2016, Maldonado was charged with leading the Chancellor's Committee for Hispanic Serving Initiatives (CCHSI), the campus effort to qualify UWM as a Hispanic Serving Institution (HSI), one with an undergraduate population that is at least 25 percent Latinx. (In 2018, Patricia Nájera Torres was appointed to serve with Maldonado as colead on UWM's HSI effort.) Between 2012 and 2014, UWM's Latinx population grew from 1,623 to 1,941. By 2017, that figure had jumped to 2,019, representing roughly 11 percent of the university's undergraduate population. By fall 2020, Latinx enrollment totaled 3,401, which included students who identify as multiethnic and Latinx, or 13.1 percent of the undergraduate student body. Given the overall decline in UWM's undergraduate student population, the continued increase of Latinx students is a notable success. Notable as well is the fact that, according to the Wisconsin Policy Forum, UWM serves the highest number of Latino college students in the area. What's more, as of 2014—the most recent date for which data are available—UWM enrolled more than a quarter of all Latinx students in the UW System.

Under Maldonado's leadership, and in collaboration with CCHSI, RHC has concentrated on meeting the growing financial needs of Latinx students by securing additional scholarships and grants and offering workshops on financial aid and academic success strategies to help students graduate faster. In response to the growing number of Deferred Action for Childhood Arrivals students on campus, RHC also began offering workshops on immigrant rights and pathways to matriculation. Continuing budget cuts, however, have led to an erosion of the center's institutional resources, including a decline in the number of support staff, advisors, and recruiters, and the loss of RHC's community outreach specialist.

Nevertheless, with the growth of Latinx enrollment at UWM, student life has flourished. Latinx students, 85 percent of whom are commuters, began seeking out social connections, in large part by joining fraternities and sororities such as Omega Delta Phi, Lambda Alpha Upsilon, Lambda Theta Phi, Gamma Alpha Omega, Zeta

Sigma Chi, and Sigma Lambda Gamma. Latinx students also became increasingly active in organizations such as Hispanic Professionals of Greater Milwaukee, Young People's Resistance Committee, and the Professional Association of Latinx for Medical School Access at the University of Wisconsin–Madison.

In 2019, RHC moved from UWM's Division of Academic Affairs to its Division of Global Inclusion & Engagement. RHC staff members who had held the title of academic advisors were instead designated multicultural student success coordinators. Although they still support students' academic progress, success coordinators provide holistic advising, with academic advisors in students' respective colleges and schools assuming responsibility for academic advising. Gabriela Dorantes, senior advisor/multicultural student success coordinator in RHC, notes the need for more advisors given the increase in the number of Latinx students on campus. She also believes UWM needs to elevate more minority staff into leadership positions. Meanwhile, with fifteen hundred Latinx students assigned to the RHC, which employs only three full-time staff members (the same number working at SSOI when it opened its doors in 1970) working under continued threats of further downsizing, the center clearly faces future challenges.

Yet today, as RHC continues to serve a growing number of Latinx students at UWM, Latinos can take pride in their contributions, over the last fifty years, to the university's vibrant research, teaching, and community service traditions. In creating the SSOI, for example, UWM

faculty and students, working with local activists, played a leading role in establishing what would become strong connections between the university and Milwaukee's Latino community. Furthermore, UWM programs in bilingual education, the social sciences, languages, creative writing, theater, and music have all been enhanced by the perspectives and experiences of the Latinx students, faculty, and staff whose presence has added immeasurably to UWM's cultural and educational diversity.

Fortunately, there is every indication that accomplishments such as these will continue to characterize the Latinx role on campus, much to the benefit of both the university and the broader city, state, and international Latino community.

# Asian Americans: A Force for Diversity, Scholarly Contributions, and Innovation

CHIA YOUYEE VANG,
LINDA HUANG, AND
ADRIAN CHAN

*Asian Faculty and Staff Association Award Ceremony at the University of Wisconsin-Milwaukee (UWM), 2017. From left to right: Tae Joon Kwak (Honorary Award, Mechanical Engineering), Shin Yoon Park (Graduate Award, Political Science), and Navee Lor (Undergraduate Award, Cell Molecular Biology).* **Photo by Susie Lamborn.**

Asia as a geographic space is expansive. At 17.2 million square miles, it's the world's largest continent. It is also the most populous, home to approximately 60 percent of the world's 7.8 billion people. Yet perhaps even more significant is Asia's rich tradition of cultural and linguistic diversity—a tradition that encompasses scores of different ethnicities. This chapter explores the identities of people of Asian descent—the fastest-growing racial group in the United States—at the University of Wisconsin-Milwaukee (UWM), as well as the paths they have traveled to join us, and the extraordinary contributions they have made and continue to make within our institution. Consider, for example, one measure of the impact of Asian Americans at UWM: today they constitute more than 54 percent of faculty members in the College of Engineering & Applied Science and more than 40 percent of faculty in the Sheldon B. Lubar School of Business.

We explore such issues within the context of the two ways the United States currently classifies people of Asian descent, classifications that have changed over time and therefore are likely to exclude some who had previously been grouped together while adding others. The US Census Bureau defines "Asians" as those who identify with one or more nationalities or ethnic groups originating in the Far East, Southeast Asia, or the Indian subcontinent. It is common in the United States to reference as "Asian American" those individuals tracing their ancestry to these regions.

Very few people of Asian descent were present at UWM prior to 1970. A review of UWM yearbooks

from 1956 to 1968 reveals only a handful of such students (in photos and with Asian surnames) during that time. In the 1956 yearbook, Agnes Yamaguchi's photo was pictured among the graduating class, L. Yamaguchi was included in a freshman group photo, and S. Singh was one of the students in the German Club photo. Although the 1957 yearbook appeared to include several Asian students, as suggested by their surnames, it was not until publication of the 1962 yearbook that the country of origin was identified for the university's foreign students; countries such as India, British North Borneo, and Korea. Campus historical data show that in fall 1971, a total of sixty "Orient-American" students were enrolled (forty-two undergraduates, twelve students pursuing master's degrees, three doctoral students, and three students designated as "special." In total, they represented 0.27 percent of the student population.

By fall 1980, the number of Orient-American students had increased to 288 (170 undergraduates, 66 master's, 17 doctoral, and 35 special students), which constituted 1.11 percent of all students. To personalize this data, it is interesting to note that Gwat-Yong Lie came from Singapore to

*Keh Tsao (left) observes a microexplosion of water and petroleum-based fuel emulsions with Chia Lik Wang, a visiting scholar from the People's Republic of China, 1984. Photo courtesy Keh Tsao.*

pursue a master's degree in social work at UWM, a degree she earned in 1980. She went on to complete a doctoral degree in social welfare from the University of Wisconsin–Madison in 1984. She taught at Arizona State University before joining UWM in 1996 as a tenured professor in the Helen Bader School of Social Welfare, eventually becoming the school's associate dean. "I felt like I was a novelty because there were so few Asian Americans on campus," said Lie, reflecting on her time as a graduate student. "I was often asked where I learned how to speak English because I spoke English very well. Truth be told, Singapore was a British colony. There were Chinese language schools and English language schools, and I went through English language schools."

One of the earliest of UWM's Asian faculty members was Hiroomi Umezawa. He had earned a PhD from Japan's Nagoya University in 1952 and taught at the University of Tokyo and the University of Naples, Italy, before joining UWM in 1966. By that time, he had become a renowned physicist for his work in quantum field theory, and his presence contributed to the establishment of UWM's physics doctoral program in 1967. Although Umezawa left UWM in 1975, he played an instrumental role in UWM's transition to a research university.

The most common path initially leading Asian faculty and staff to UWM was the desire to study in the United States. Like Lie, the late Victor Chou, associate professor of economics; Tong Hun Lee, professor emeritus of economics; and Keh Tsao, professor emeritus of mechanical engineering, all came to this country as students and decided to remain. All three earned their graduate degrees from UW–Madison and accepted positions at other US institutions before being recruited to UWM (Lee and Tsao in 1967 and Chou in 1969), where they remained throughout their careers. Lee, who came to UWM from the University of Tennessee, served on the faculty for twenty-nine years. Tsao joined UWM as a visiting associate professor after teaching for six years at the South Dakota School of Mines and Technology, remaining until his 1995 retirement. Recalled Tsao, "I was the only faculty member of Asian descent in the Engineering College

in 1967." After earning his doctorate in 1953, Chou served as chief economist for the Allis-Chalmers Corporation before most likely becoming the first Asian professor in what was then UWM's School of Business Administration in 1969, where he remained until his death in 1989.

Other early Asian faculty were born in the United States. They included Adrian Chan, professor emeritus of educational psychology, a second-generation Chinese American who joined UWM in the fall of 1968 during a time of racial unrest in Milwaukee and remained at UWM until his retirement in 2000. "At that time, my graduate training in clinical and counseling psychology did not prepare me for the urban issues I was facing," said Chan, referring to his early years at UWM. "It was a new learning experience for me . . . so I had to develop new models of learning, teaching, and dealing with the multicultural communities. My connections to the Milwaukee community were mostly with the African American, Latino/Latina, and American Indian groups." Chan was one of the first Asian American diversity leaders at UWM, serving as assistant vice-chancellor in what was then the Office for Multicultural Affairs from 1991 to 1995.

As UWM expanded its academic programs in the 1970s, more Asian faculty members were recruited. Yoshio Niho (Japanese), Abbas Husayn Hamdani (Indian), and Swarnjit Arora (Indian) were among these early arrivals. Niho and Arora both joined the Department of Economics—Niho in 1970 and Arora in 1972—and went on to have long, impactful careers at UWM. (Niho retired in

*UWM's Adrian Chan (right) in South Africa with Archbishop Desmond Tutu, 1995.* Photo courtesy Adrian Chan. ▶

*Tong Hun Lee, Yoshio Niho, Satya Das, and Melvin Louise (left to right) with Swarnjit Arora's family at Milwaukee's Lake Park, 1981.* Photo courtesy Swarnjit Arora.

2008 and Arora in 2018.) Arora recalled what it was like when he first joined the faculty, noting that "I arrived shortly after the PhD program in economics was approved. Even though there were only a handful of Asians on campus, UWM was a welcoming place for me. Everyone wanted to know about me, India, and Sikhs. They had never met a person with a turban before. I was invited by presidents of corporations to speak, and I was interviewed on TV many times." Hamdani, a renowned teacher and writer of Middle Eastern and Islamic history and philosophy, was recruited by the Department of History, where he taught from 1970 until his retirement in 2001. The recipient of many awards for his teaching and service, Hamdani cofounded the Islamic Christian Dialogue in Milwaukee, which became internationally known, in large part for inspiring a new generation of interfaith leaders.

Staff of Asian descent were also a rarity at UWM during this period. When Emraida Kiram joined what was then the Department of Registration and Records in 1976, only one other Filipina worked in the same building. Recalled Kiram, "Since I was in charge of the work study students in the department, one of my first contacts at UWM was with African American students. They taught me how to work with Black students and to not be afraid." Kiram, who for a time worked as a supervisor in the Registrar's Office, fondly described how meaningful it was to interact with such individuals as Ernest Spaights, at the time an assistant chancellor and faculty member dedicated to removing racial barriers to student success. Kiram remained on the job for thirty-four years.

Although Asian student enrollment continued to increase during this time frame, it would be fall 1984 before it exceeded three hundred students, and one year more before the university changed the "Orient-American" category to "Asian American" in its enrollment charts. To distinguish between domestic and foreign-born students, the National Center for Education Statistics in 1976 began requiring that a student who was not a citizen or national of the United States be reported as a "nonresident alien." Consequently, UWM began to

*Swarnjit Arora participating in a television interview, 1973.* Photo courtesy Swarnjit Arora.

Linda Huang (fifth from right in blue sweater) with multicultural staff in Bolton Hall.
Photo courtesy Linda Huang.

place foreign Asian students in a new category it termed "International."

The Wisconsin State Legislature's definition of minority undergraduates in 1985 included Asians, but only those who had arrived in the United States after 1975 and could trace their origins to Southeast Asia. Four years later, yet another change in labeling occurred when the University of Wisconsin System approved a new category, "South East Asian," for the ninety-eight students on campus who were Cambodian, Hmong, Lao, or Vietnamese, and whose families came to the United States as refugees following the Vietnam War. (The terminology "Other Asian" was used to identify the remaining 356 students.)

Because Asian Americans were collectively no longer considered underrepresented in higher education, the rationale for the new category was meant to ensure that this subgroup of students could access support resources available to other historically underrepresented populations. Indeed, by 1990, the Asian American student population at UWM had increased to 507 (93 categorized as South East Asian and 414 as Asian American), constituting 2 percent of the student body. Ten years later, that number had nearly doubled (414 South East Asian and 469 Asian American, and nearly 4 percent of all students) due in part to the burgeoning number of Southeast Asian students.

By the 1980s, Asians in US society were being viewed as the so-called "model minority." The stereotypical view many held (and continue to hold) of Asian students—as incredibly smart, hard

working, and so focused they do not need support services—became a common perception. Yet, contradicting the model minority myth, was the fact that many Southeast Asian students were former refugees with widely varying educational backgrounds, some of whom needed additional support to thrive.

To be sure, as the number of Southeast Asian students continued to grow, students and community members began advocating for greater support services. During the 1988–1989 school year, College of Letters and Science Assistant Dean Erland F. Olfe tasked Patty Cobb, an advisor in the college, with exploring the need for targeted advising services for Southeast Asian students like those that had been established for their African American, Latino, and Native American peers. Cobb reached out to Ronald Podeschi, at the time a professor in the School of Education who—motivated by the incredible sacrifices that Hmong, Laotian, Vietnamese, and Cambodian people had made in the Vietnam War—was already heavily involved with Milwaukee's Southeast Asian community. Cobb also consulted high school guidance counselors in Milwaukee Public Schools, interviewed Southeast Asian students, and surveyed community group members. She quickly ascertained that there was, indeed, significant need for advising services, and Southeast Asian Student Academic Services (SASAS) was launched in 1991 with Cobb as its first coordinator.

Hmong staff members such as Lang Her (and later, Tong Her) were among those who worked in SASAS, advising Southeast Asian students. They were succeeded in 1997 by Dao Vang, who had arrived at UWM ten years earlier to begin his doctoral studies in economics. Witnessing his fellow Southeast Asian students' need for additional support, Vang joined others to advocate for such resources. He also helped establish the Hmong Student Association, becoming its first president during the 1989–1990 school year. By 1998, Vang had been promoted to the position of SASAS coordinator, which in 2006 was renamed Southeast Asian American Student Academic Services (SAASAS) to be inclusive of the increasing number of American-born students of Southeast Asian descent. SAASAS was moved from the College of Letters & Science to the Division of Academic Affairs in 2017. Three years later, it became the Southeast Asian American Student Center (SEAASC), joining UWM's other multicultural student centers in what was then the Division of Global Inclusion & Engagement. Vang served as SEAASC lead until he retired in 2021.

In 2000, SASAS hired its (and perhaps UWM's) first Lao academic staff member, Channy "Johnny" Rasavong. He recalled his work with SASAS over the course of eighteen years as rewarding: "The position connected me to the Lao students on campus and the Lao community in Milwaukee," said Rasavong. "I have been committed to student success by supporting them [in their efforts] to persist and graduate."

For each year between 1976—when Emraida Kiram arrived at UWM—and the late 1990s, the percentage of Asian American staff members never

Patty Cobb (right) and Tong Her, the first two Southeast Asian staff members in what was then Student Academic Services, early 1990s. Photo courtesy Dao Vang.

exceeded 0.2 percent. That scenario meant that Academic Staff Emerita Linda Huang, who had joined UWM in April 1989, worked primarily with African American, Latino/Latina, and American Indian faculty, staff, and students. (In fact, it was Ricardo Fernández, at the time assistant vice-chancellor in the Division of Academic Affairs and coordinator of the division's newly established M/D [Multicultural/Disadvantaged] Office, who had hired Huang.) "Throughout my professional career at UWM," Huang recalled, "I have consistently worked with multicultural students and assisted in the campus-wide diversity efforts. I have witnessed the evolution of multicultural offices over the years."

In contrast to the relatively slow growth in the number of staff and students of Asian descent at UWM, the number of Asian faculty members increased more quickly, totaling 78 by the end of the twentieth century and representing 10.8

Dao Vang (standing in back) with new students sharing academic success experiences, 2003. Front row, left to right: Pachoua Thao, Hue Vang, Steve Xiong, Xue Cha, and Ka Kelly Yang. Photo courtesy Dao Vang.

*Pradeep Rohatgi (front row, second from left) with UWM scholarship winners at the American Foundry Society Regional Casting Competition, 2018.* Photo courtesy Pradeep Rohatgi.

percent of all 724 faculty members. Their presence was most visible in the disciplines of science, technology, engineering, and mathematics (STEM). Two of the many individuals who came to UWM in the 1980s and made significant contributions over the decades were Devarajan Venugopalan, associate vice-chancellor in the Division of Academic Affairs; and Pradeep Rohatgi, distinguished professor of materials science and engineering. After completing his doctoral degree at McMaster University in Canada, Venugopalan joined the College of Engineering & Applied Science as a materials engineering professor in fall 1984. He recalled that even as the chair of the Computer Science Department introduced himself to Venugopalan and put him in contact with people in the community, "It felt strange as other faculty members checked out my English-speaking skills, [saying], 'Your English seems to be okay. You should be able to handle classes.'"

One year later, Venugopalan was joined at UWM by Pradeep Rohatgi, who had earned a doctorate from the Massachusetts Institute of Technology in 1964, worked in industry in the United States and India, served as a professor at the Indian Institute of Science in Bangalore and at the Indian Institute of Technology in Kanpur, and established two national research labs in India. Rohatgi explained how he came to UWM:

> There was a big gas accident in the lab at Bhopal earlier in the year. Since things were unstable, we moved here in July 1985. Basically, the idea was to stay here for a

while until the lab had been cleaned up and then return. I was brought in as a full tenured professor. I was informed that I was here to help establish research and contribute to the research profile because I had established two national labs. I was to do research that would be relevant to the State of Wisconsin, because that's what kinds of labs I started in India, [labs] that responded to the needs of the region. In the beginning when I started to talk to industry, they said, "We didn't know that UWM did any research. We thought that it was just a teaching school."

In the late 1980s and through the 1990s, steps were taken to add more women and individuals from historically underrepresented groups to UWM's faculty. That move, along with a simultaneous desire to emphasize global diversity, led to the increase in the number of Asian faculty members. Take, for example, Alice Kuramoto, professor emerita of nursing. A third-generation Japanese American (i.e, a sansei), Kuramoto was recruited to UWM by Betty Mitsunaga, an associate dean in the School of Nursing. Both Mitsunaga and Kuramoto had been on the faculty at the University of Washington in Seattle (where Kuramoto also served as an associate dean) before Mitsunaga left to join the University of Colorado prior to coming to UWM in 1984. Recalled Kuramoto, "I moved to Milwaukee on Christmas Day 1988 and Betty picked me up at the airport on that snowy day and invited me to her home for dinner." Kuramoto began her tenure at UWM as a visiting professor in January

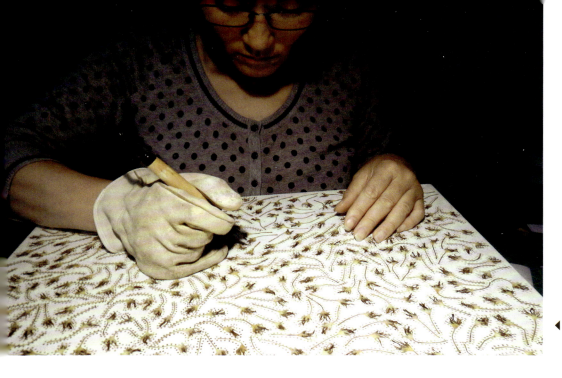

1989, staying until her retirement in 2001. "It is interesting that I had more of an Asian experience here in Milwaukee than in Seattle," she continued. "When I came . . . we had an Indian woman who was an assistant professor, a Filipina associate, Betty Mitsunaga, myself, and then another woman who was a Japanese clinical instructor. There were five of us Asian women just in the nursing school in 1989, so that's pretty impressive."

Several faculty members hired during the 1990s recalled similar paths. After serving as a research associate at the Medical College of Virginia, Hanh Trinh joined UWM's Department of Health Informatics and Administration. Trinh, most likely UWM's first Vietnamese American faculty member, had fled Vietnam in 1975 as a refugee. He recalled being "welcomed by my colleagues when arriving at the university in 1994," adding that "I was lucky to have a lot of support from wonderful colleagues who shared with me their own experiences of the academic life on campus. I met many Asian scholars who welcomed me to their network."

Susie Lamborn, an associate professor of educational psychology, is a second-generation Japanese American born in New Jersey and raised in Pennsylvania. After completing her graduate studies at the University of Denver, she served as a postdoctoral fellow at the University of California, Irvine, and as a researcher at the University of West Florida before accepting an assistant professor position at UWM in 1995. Recalled Lamborn, "At that time, I spent a lot of time by myself. It was Dr. Adrian Chan, who was a faculty [member] in

the department and knew everyone, who introduced me to other people on campus."

Like many of her peers born and raised in Taiwan, Yea-Fen Chen went abroad for graduate school, attending Indiana University where she earned a doctoral degree in foreign language education. Chen recalled that her 1998 interview for a Chinese language visiting professor position at UWM included a teaching demonstration, an overnight stay with then-Professor of History David Buck and his family, and a visit to the Milwaukee Art Museum. "When I got the job offer, I was excited to take it because of the pleasant campus visit I had," said Chen, who would go on to play a key role in developing the Chinese language program at UWM. She earned tenure before leaving UWM for Indiana University in 2013.

Kyoung Ae Cho, professor of art and design, joined UWM's Peck School of the Arts (PSOA) in 1999 as an assistant professor. Born in South Korea, Cho came to the United States to pursue graduate studies at Cranbrook Academy of Art in Bloomfield Hills, Michigan. She had not planned to stay in the United States beyond graduate school, but many opportunities presented themselves that made it difficult to leave. Regarding her experiences as a faculty of Asian descent, Cho said, "I was the only Asian in our department when I was hired, and I am still the only tenured Asian faculty member. There has been a part-time Asian instructor from time to time. But with very caring and supportive colleagues, and also with a busy schedule, there wasn't any time to be feeling that I am different."

| YEAR | STUDENTS (Undergraduate & Graduate) | STAFF | FACULTY |
|---|---|---|---|
| 2010 | 1,467 → 4.8% | 111 → 3.9% | 145 → 16.7% |
| 2020 | 1,347 → 5.8%* | 132 → 4.7%* | 150 → 20.5% |

*Sources: UWM Office of Assessment and Institutional Research and Department of Human Resources.*
**Excludes students enrolled at UWM branch campuses as of 2018.*

The reason for the significant growth in the number of Asian faculty members can be traced to UWM's commitment to recruiting prominent and emerging Asian scholars, such as Kumkum Sangari, the William F. Vilas Research Professor of English and the Humanities; Chia Youyee Vang, professor of history; and Shinji Takahashi, senior lecturer in foreign languages and literature.

Prior to coming to UWM in 2004, Sangari had been a professorial fellow at the Centre for Contemporary Studies, Nehru Memorial Museum and Library, New Delhi, and a visiting professor at the University of Chicago and Central European University in Budapest. In discussing the reasons she has remained in Milwaukee, Sangari recalled that "when I came to UWM, I discovered that the students here were mostly working class. Most of them were not getting family support and were working to support themselves. They were so gritty. The fact that some were quite brilliant, and very hard working, I think that was something that has kept me here. It's actually the fact that, for them, learning matters."

Vang arrived in the United States as a refugee from Laos in 1980. She was completing her graduate studies at the University of Minnesota when the History Department recruited her to UWM in fall 2006. "Faculty members, such as Gregory Jay and Rachel Buff, had supported Hmong students' request for greater inclusion," recalled Vang. "The Cultures and Communities Program provided funding for the Hmong American Studies Initiative that was led by Mary Louise Buley-Meissner, at the time a professor of English, and Vincent Her, who was then a doctoral student in cultural anthropology. It was these advocacy efforts by students and faculty that resulted in my hire, so I've taught in both history and comparative ethnic studies over the years."

Takahashi came to UWM from Japan in 2008 because his wife hailed from Wisconsin. Hired to teach Japanese, he has been instrumental in expanding the College of Letters & Science's Japanese program to include activities such as a Japanese speech contest for heritage speakers and adult learners, and Japan Bowl, a national competition on Japanese trivia for high school students.

▲

*Members of the Asian Faculty and Staff Association (AFSA) Steering Committee, 2019. Front row left to right: Janey Christofferson, Pachoua Lor, Natalie Chin; Back row left to right: Swarnjit Arora, Vipavee Thongpriwan, Gwat-Yong Lie, Yuko Kojima Wert, Karen Miyoshi, and Channy "Johnny" Rasavong. Photo courtesy Susie Lamborn.*

*UWM Korea Day Concert with (left to right): Bomsori Kim, guest violinist; Jong-kook Lee, consul-general, Republic of Korea; and organizing committee members, 2017.* Photo courtesy Kyoung Ae Cho.

As mentioned earlier, Gwat-Yong Lie had been a student at UWM during the 1970s. Although there were more Asians on campus by the time she joined UWM as an associate professor in 1996, she noted that even then "there was no Asian collective and very little recognition of the contributions that we were making on campus." Indeed, in the early 1990s, Alice Kuramoto had reached out to other Asian faculty and staff who had begun meeting for informal lunch discussions in a quest for mutual support. Three years later, it had become clear that having an affinity group was important. Yet it was still 2002 before the Asian Faculty and Staff Association (AFSA) was founded to advocate and create networking opportunities among Asian Americans on campus. Lie was selected as AFSA's first chair. Other members of the AFSA Steering Committee were Swarnjit Arora, Hanh Quang Trinh, Linda Huang, Susie Lamborn, Hur-Li Lee, Alice Kuramoto, and C. J. Kim. In addition to supporting its members, AFSA established an

*Satya Nadella, chairman and CEO, Microsoft Corporation.*
Photo courtesy Microsoft Corporation.

awards program that has recognized forty-five Asian undergraduates, graduate students, and PhD candidates for their achievements since 2004.

Over the years, other affinity groups were organized, such as the Korean Faculty Group, now the Korean American Faculty and Staff Association. Cho recalled that in 2014 she and four other Korean faculty members (Sun Sunwoong Kim, Jun Kim, Jaejin Jang, and Sooyeon Lee) reorganized UWM's Korea Day event, scheduling it to coincide with the opening concert of the PSOA orchestra and a performance by a top-notch Korean soloist. Since 2016, the Korean American Association of Milwaukee has cohosted the event through which organizers share Korean culture across campus and with the greater Milwaukee community.

Student organizations also have been instrumental in community building among Asian Americans. Such groups include the Asian Student Union, Graduate Organization of Asian Pacific Islander Students, Hmong Student Association, Chinese Club, Japanese Culture Association, Students of India Association, and Vietnamese Student Association. Many students of Asian descent who attended UWM have gone on to make significant contributions to society. One of the most prominent is Microsoft Chairman and CEO Satya Nadella, who earned a master's degree in computer science in 1990. Another notable alumnus is Hong Kong politician Wu Chi-wai, a former leader of Hong Kong's biggest opposition party who is currently in detention and the recipient of a master's degree in economics in 1991. Still another alumnus of note is the Filipino writer Jose Dalisay Jr., recipient of a PhD in English in 1991.

*Ava Udvadia, associate professor of biological sciences and recipient of the University of Wisconsin System's 2021 Regent Scholar Award.*

When reviewing the larger social impact of people of Asian descent at UWM, additional contributions stand out:

○ — In 1972, Keh Tsao established the world's first air quality measurement laboratory at UWM with a grant from the Wisconsin Department of Natural Resources. Tsao's graduate students managed this lab, which monitored continuous air quality, until his retirement in 1995.

○ — Research and scholarship of early Asian faculty members, primarily in economics and several STEM fields, substantially contributed to the university's recognition as a Research I university by the Carnegie Classification of Institutions of Higher Education.

○ — The UWM Graduate School's record of top researchers from 1993 to 2003 included 17 Asian faculty members, accounting for 17 percent of its top researchers. Together, this group was awarded more than $12 million of extramural research grants. The trend has continued, with 16.5 percent of UWM grant funds going to Asian American researchers in fiscal year 2021.

○ — As of spring 2021, Asian American faculty were concentrated in and made up a significant percentage of the total faculty in several colleges/schools:

   · 54.1 percent of the 61 faculty in the College of Engineering & Applied Science;
   · 35.3 percent of the 17 faculty in the School of Information Studies;
   · 41.7 percent of the 48 faculty in the Sheldon B. Lubar School of Business; and
   · 17.8 percent of the faculty in the College of Letters & Science.

○ — Throughout the years, a number of Asian-related academic programs have contributed to curriculum diversification at UWM: Asian Studies and Hmong Diaspora Studies certificates; Chinese, Japanese, and Korean majors; and a number of cultural/linguistic courses. Such efforts have enabled UWM students to graduate into a world that demands knowledge of the cultures, economies, and histories of Asia, a region that currently plays a dominant role in the global economic, diplomatic, and cultural landscape.

○ — Many Asian faculty have contributed to the expansion of UWM's global outreach by leading short-term study abroad programs to various parts of Asia, assisting in the recruitment of students from Asian countries, and hosting international conferences.

● — A number of awards were established for students and faculty, including the Asian Faculty and Staff Association Award (to recognize Asian students for academic excellence and contributions to Milwaukee's Asian community); the Dr. Swarnjit Arora Award (to underwrite a scholarship for undergraduate and graduate students of Asian descent); the Niho Faculty Excellence Fund (established by Professor Emeritus of Economics Yoshio Niho to support research in the Department of Economics); the Dr. Alice Kuramoto Scholarship (to support doctoral Hmong students in nursing); the Organization of Chinese Americans-Wisconsin Chapter Scholarship (to support students active in Asian American communities); the Kanti Prasad Student and Faculty Talent Fund (to recognize junior faculty scholarly achievement and outstanding members of the senior class, and underwrite scholarships for business students); and the Victor Chou Scholarship (established by Chou's family to support seniors majoring in finance with demonstrated financial need).

*Yea-Fen Chen (center back row holding child) with students in Taiwan, 2004.*
Photo courtesy Yea-Fen Chen.

*Shinji Takahashi (far right) with students in Japan, 2018.*
Photo courtesy Shinji Takahashi.

● — Of the sixty faculty members who since 1973 have achieved UWM Distinguished Professor status in recognition of their significant impact on their fields, five are of Asian descent. Uk Heo, in political science, and Pradeep Rohatgi, in materials engineering, are currently on the faculty. Heo, a scholar renowned for his deep expertise on Korean political and security affairs, has written extensively on the North Korean nuclear crisis and US-South Korean relations. Rohatgi is the recipient of numerous international awards for excellence in research. He has coauthored more than four hundred scientific research papers and seventy papers on science and society and owns twenty US patents. Junhong Chen, in mechanical engineering, was named one of the world's most cited academic researchers in the field of materials science in 2017 and 2018 by Clarivate Analytics, an information service and analytics company serving the scientific research community. He left UWM in 2019 to join the faculty at the University of Chicago. Arun Garg, in industrial manufacturing engineering, and David Tong, in physics, are retired.

*Alice Kuramoto presents the Dr. Alice Kuramoto Scholarship to Hmong graduate nursing student Bao Xiong, 2017. Photo courtesy Alice Kuramoto.*

*Uk Heo engaging with students in a graduate seminar, 2018.* Photo by Chia Youyee Vang.

*Devarajan Venugopalan, UWM's associate vice-chancellor for academic affairs since 2005.*

*Vice-Chancellor for Diversity, Equity, and Inclusion Chia Youyee Vang, 2022.*

○ — In 2020, a total of 10 of UWM's 59 scientists ranked in the top 2 percent in their fields (based on the frequency of citation of their work during their careers) were Asian Americans.

○ — A small number of Asian Americans have held administrative leadership positions at UWM. One of the first was Betty Mitsunaga, who served as associate dean in the School of Nursing in the 1980s. Devarajan Venugopalan was associate dean in the College of Engineering & Applied Science from 1998 to 2004. For a long time, he was the only person of Asian descent to serve as an associate vice-chancellor—in his case, in the Division of Academic Affairs—a position he accepted in 2005 and still holds today.

In 2017, Chia Youyee Vang was appointed associate vice-chancellor in the Division of Global Inclusion & Engagement— renamed the Division of Diversity, Equity, and Inclusion (DEI) in August 2021—becoming the second Asian American to serve the campus at this level. Vang's March 2021 appointment as UWM's interim chief DEI officer and appointment as vice-chancellor for DEI in January 2022 made her the first Asian American cabinet member in UWM's history.

Other Asian American academic and administrative leaders include the following:

○ — Adrian Chan, assistant vice-chancellor, Office for Multicultural Affairs, 1991–1995;

○ — V. Kanti Prasad, associate dean, Sheldon B. Lubar School of Business, 1978–1998; interim dean, 2001–2002; and dean, 2002–2009 and 2015–2019;

○ — Alan Shoho, dean of the School of Education, 2015–2020;

○ — Kaushal Chari, dean of the Sheldon B. Lubar School of Business, 2019 to the present;

*Alan Shoho, dean, School of Education, 2015–2020.*

*Kaushal Chari, dean, Sheldon B. Lubar School of Business, 2020.*

*Gwat-Yong Lie speaking at an AFSA reception, 2017.*
Photo courtesy Susie Lamborn.

● — Wooseob Jeong, interim dean, School of Information Studies, 2012–2014;

● — Gwat-Yong Lie, associate dean, Academic Programs & Student Services, Graduate School, 2004–2009; interim dean, Graduate School, 2006–2007; interim associate dean, School of Information Studies, 2010–2012; interim associate dean, Helen Bader School of Social Welfare (HBSSW), 2011–2013; and associate dean, HBSSW, 2013–2021; and

● — David Yu, associate dean for graduate study, College of Engineering & Applied Science (CEAS), 2009–2013; interim dean, Graduate School, 2011–2012; and interim associate dean of research, CEAS, 2018–2019.

Asian American faculty, staff, and students have traveled diverse paths to UWM over the last sixty-five years. They have undoubtedly played a significant role both in diversifying the university's workforce and student populations and in advancing its research profile. What's more, alumni have found ways to support their alma mater. For example, a recent $2 million gift from alumnus Satya Nadella and his wife, Anupama, that created the Fund for Diversity in Tech Education at UWM, epitomizes the impact that a UWM experience can have on students. If past trends are an indication of what the future holds, Asian Americans at UWM will continue to make important contributions to the university campus and beyond.

## CHAPTER 5

# Women at UWM: Decades of Activism, Fragile Gains

GWYNNE KENNEDY AND
MERRY WIESNER-HANKS

*University of Wisconsin-Milwaukee (UWM) graduates celebrating at Gradfest, May 2021.*
*Left to right: Ana Cruz, Joy Tropp, Valerie Gorospe, Jennifer Bahena, and Zuleyka Albiter.*

Women students, staff, and faculty at UWM have long worked on a group of core issues that have remained strikingly similar: safety and security; sexual harassment and assault; childcare and family leave; increased research and teaching about women, gender, and sexuality; equity in pay, tenure, and promotion; readily available data for accountability; and campus climate on diversity issues. They have also sought to increase the number, visibility, and chances for success of women faculty and staff, administrators, and student leaders. Women have formed organizations that connected with community groups and initiated services later adopted by the university, including an after-dark ride service, more extensive health care, support for international students, special services for older students, a faculty mentoring program, and orientation for new faculty and staff.

Women made up about a third of the students and faculty at UWM when it began as an institution in 1956. By 1978, they accounted for more than half of both undergraduates and graduates,

and by 1999, almost half of those receiving PhDs. By contrast, the number of women faculty fell during UWM's early years—from about a third to about a fifth—and then climbed slowly, reaching the 1956 level again only in 2001. Over its entire history as an institution, UWM has had one woman chancellor, two women provosts, and eleven women who served as academic deans in its now fifteen schools and colleges, including six in nursing.

The fifteen years from 1956 to 1971 were years of expansion for UWM in terms of students, faculty, and programs. After falling for several years after 1956, the percentage of women in the student body began to climb, reaching 43 percent in 1970; however, the share of women faculty fell to about 20 percent in 1970 and then stayed there, reflecting the sharp gender dichotomy nationally in graduate education. The only senior women administrators were the deans in what was then the School of Nursing, and the Dean of Women, a position held by Charlotte Wollaeger from 1936 to 1960.

One early women's organization on campus was the Women's League, which began the same year as UWM and continued into the 1980s. It brought together women faculty and staff and the wives of male faculty members. The Women's League offered scholarships to students and organized luncheons and groups for women with different interests. It also created events and services that were later picked up by the university, their origins as women's projects forgotten. These included First Fridays, the once-a-month cocktail hour for faculty and staff from across campus; a dinner honoring retirees; an orientation for new

The UWM Day Care Center,
The Committee On the Status of Academic Women,
The Equal Opportunity Office,

and the
UWM Women's League
cordially invite you to attend the

October "First Friday" to celebrate

the 10th anniversary of the UWM Day Care Center

October 2, 1981, 4:30-7:00 P.M.

UWM Union                    Hors d'oeuvres
Wisconsin Room Lounge        Cash bar

◀ *Invitation to a First Friday event at UWM, 1981.*

specialty for which UWM became widely known. The vast majority of faculty in the School of Nursing were women, as were its students. The steady rise in the number of women students at UWM from the 1960s was due in part to the excellent reputation of the School of Nursing, today the College of Nursing and the largest nursing program in Wisconsin.

In the late 1960s, groups that were part of the movement for women's rights pressured the federal government to prohibit sex-based discrimination, which it did through executive orders and civil rights laws such as Title IX, which was enacted in 1972. Universities began to appoint affirmative action officers and other advisors charged with monitoring the status of women. Lenore W. Harmon, director of the UWM Counseling Center and later a professor in the Department of Educational Psychology, was named advisor to the chancellor on the status of women in 1971. Harmon, however, declined to continue in the position the following year, commenting that she had no substantive duties and seemed to be in the post just to make the administration look good.

faculty; and welcome lunches and a supply room for international students.

The one exception to this very male story was nursing, which began as a program attached to the University of Wisconsin School of Nursing and became an independent School of Nursing in 1965. Frances H. Cunningham was the key figure facilitating the transition. (Cunningham Hall, built in 1973 to house the School of Nursing, is named after her.) Under the leadership of its first dean, Inez G. Hinsvark, and Cunningham as associate dean, the School of Nursing established a strong baccalaureate program accredited in 1969, recruited a faculty with nationally prominent scholars, and initiated a master's-level Community Health Nursing Program, a

*Women's Week flyer, 1973.*
Photo by Alan Magayne-Roshak.

Pressure for change at academic institutions across the country on women's issues came not only from the federal government, but also from students, staff, and faculty. Beginning in the early 1970s, women students formed several action groups. They opened the Campus Women's Information Center in 1972, reorganized and renamed the Feminist Center in 1974. It maintained a staffed room in the UWM Student Union that provided information, referrals, and a resource library; organized speakers, concerts, and workshops; and ran consciousness-raising sessions and self-defense training. To highlight the objectification of women, the Women's Information Center sponsored

▶

"Mr. Man Contest" winner John Lindquist, a Vietnam War veteran, receiving his roses, 1973. Photo by Alan Magayne-Roshak.

a "Mr. Man" contest, complete with evening wear and swimsuits; the winner's prizes included twenty-five dollars, a half barrel of beer, and a bunch of red roses. In 1975, Feminist Center leaders sent a letter to UWM faculty calling out the generic "man," "he," "mankind," and similar sexist language, and suggesting instead terms such as "person" and "they." Faculty responses included several that pointed out the students' one usage error and scolded them for everything from the age of their typewriter ribbon to their presumption. After surveying more than one thousand UWM students about their contraceptive practices and preferences, the Feminist Center attempted to change campus policies to enable students to get contraceptives at the Student Health Center, which would make them more accessible and possibly cheaper. The Feminist Center shared an office in the Student Union with the Pro-Choice Abortion Coalition, established in 1976 to defend a woman's right to an abortion as guaranteed by the 1973 US Supreme Court ruling in Roe v. Wade. It provided information and referrals to students, sponsored several discussion series and fund-raising events for local groups, and carried out lobbying and demonstrations in support of a woman's right to choose.

In a move to improve women's safety on and near campus in 1976, students from the Feminist Center started the Women's Transit Service, a ride service staffed entirely by volunteers that offered rides from campus to women after dark. Attempting to increase diversity in student government, Students for Positive Change (SPC) ran a slate of candidates that included Black men

and women, white women, and Latinx students in the 1978–1979 UWM Student Association elections. According to SPC member Lori Vance, some SPC candidates were Vietnam War veterans who voiced the needs of older students. SPC defeated the all-white, mostly male Zephyr slate. Vance became the first director of the Women's Caucus within the Student Association, which in 1978 sponsored an Affirmative Action Day Rally and other events, started a Whistlestop program to encourage women to carry whistles for use in case of attack, and—using affirmative action data—wrote letters to chairs, deans, and division heads at UWM about hiring women for open positions.

In 1971, faculty, academic staff, and students formed the Ad Hoc Committee on the Status of Academic Women (CSAW), a grassroots organization that at times included more than one hundred members. The designation "ad hoc" was dropped in 1975 when the committee saw the extent of work before them. CSAW quickly

◀ US Representative Bella Abzug and Women's Caucus student at Affirmative Action Day, 1979.

▲

*Members of the Committee on the Status of Academic Women, 1977. Front row, left to right: Janet Dunleavy, Jane Crisler, Lenore Harmon, and Carole Shammas; back row, left to right: Mary Conway, Cecilia Ridgeway, Marilyn Moon, Ethel Sloane, Marian Swoboda, and Rachel I. Skalitzky.*

established a significant presence on campus: working to elect more women to university committees, serving as the core of the 1975–1976 Title IX Institutional Self-Evaluation Task Force, weighing in on cases where women were denied tenure, developing an informal mentoring program, advocating for a program in women's studies and a campus day care center, and pushing for the appointment of more women and minorities to search and screen committees, and for better and more open compilation of data on faculty and staff by race and gender. The committee held events for campus women and sponsored two well-attended, day-long conferences in the community designed to introduce UWM to adult women contemplating entering or returning to college. In 1985, CSAW renamed itself the Association of Women in Education (AWE) to reflect its efforts to open membership to all women at UWM. AWE, which continued until 1996, offered a wide range of programs and funded a graduate scholarship. As past AWE Presidents Kim Romenesko and Pat Kissinger recall, AWE meetings were the one place where women across campus and job status could gather, network, and come to know each other.

Childcare was an important issue for students, faculty, and staff. In 1971, Students for Childcare (later named the Coalition for Campus Childcare) pushed for, planned, and then opened a small day care center in two rooms in Vogel Hall, staffed by paid and volunteer students and available only to students. One of those students was Pamela Boulton, who would go on to be the director of the Child Care Center (now the Children's Learning Center) for over forty years. In 1974, it moved to what had been the campus elementary lab school, in a building later named after Ethel Wright Kunkle, a longtime member of the Department of Educational Psychology who specialized in early childhood education. Over the years, the Child Care Center grew from about fifty children its first year

to close to three hundred, and expanded availability to faculty, staff, and members of the UWM Alumni Association. Boulton designed a curriculum in the School of Education for childcare providers that included credit courses in program development, leadership, and childcare administration; the program was later split between the School of Education and the School of Continuing Education. The Child Care Center was recognized nationally for its innovative and excellent programming and was the first provider in Milwaukee to be accredited by the National Association for the Education of Young Children. By the time Boulton retired in 2011, the center's initial budget of just under $30,000 had grown to $3.2 million.

Title IX provisions prohibiting sex-based discrimination included athletics, and women's teams were supposed to receive equal support. That did not happen, although women athletes and coaches gradually received greater recognition. The first woman—Nancy Ehrke, for swimming and diving—was inducted into the UWM Athletics Hall of Fame in 1984, twelve years after this honor was established, and the first woman coach—M. A. Kelling, who coached women's basketball from 1978 to 1995—was inducted in 2000. UWM women's basketball teams were league regular season champions in 2000–2001 and league tournament champions in 2005–2006.

One of the primary goals of women's groups on campus was the creation of a program in women's studies. An informal list of courses with women's studies content first appeared in 1972; both students and CSAW members collected

◄ *UWM women's basketball, 1978.*
Photo by Alan Magayne-Roshak.

One of the most popular women's studies courses was Ethel Sloane's Biology of Women, which she taught in a huge classroom for many years. The course became the basis of Sloane's textbook *Biology of Women,* first published in 1980, and still in print forty years later in a sixth edition revised by Theresa M. Hornstein and Jeri Lynn Schwerin. Widely praised for combining biological depth for medical professionals with readability for non-major students, the book contained photos of women from Milwaukee's Bread and Roses Women's Health Center as illustrations of women confronting reproductive and health issues.

The School of Nursing remained a leader in the UW System and beyond. In 1973, UWM began to appoint, as Distinguished Professors, senior faculty with international reputations who had made a significant impact on their fields. The first two women were both from nursing: Helen Creighton, a nurse attorney with expertise in the legal aspects of nursing, and Harriet H. Werley,

information, urged curricular development, held open meetings, and developed a program. The Office of Women's Studies was formally established in February 1974, making UWM the first campus in the UW System to have a women's studies program; UW–Madison's program came one year later.

Lenore Harmon became the first program coordinator, but she resigned fairly quickly. Rachel I. Skalitzky, then an assistant professor in the Department of Comparative Literature, was appointed to succeed her, remaining coordinator until 1983. Students could major in women's studies through the interdisciplinary major, or, after 1978, enroll in an eighteen-credit-hour interdisciplinary certificate program, which became the largest certificate program at UWM. There were no instructional funds or faculty lines, so courses were offered by departments; by 1977, about thirty to thirty-five courses with 100 percent women's studies content were offered each year, in several schools. Other positive developments for women's studies included the continued growth in library holdings, thanks to the efforts of Edi (Edith) Bjorklund, head of acquisitions at UWM's Golda Meir Library. UWM also assumed a prominent role in the establishment of statewide, regional, and national organizations in women's studies.

*Professor of Biology Ethel Sloane with her famous textbook,*
Biology of Women, *1980.* ▶

## Distinguished Professors:

| | | |
|---|---|---|
| Helen Creighton | Nursing | 1978 |
| Harriet H. Werley | Nursing | 1983 |
| Jane Gallop | English | 1992 |
| Joan Moore | Sociology | 1994 |
| Patricia Mellencamp | Art History | 1997 |
| Merry Wiesner-Hanks | History | 2007 |
| Margaret Atherton | Philosophy | 2007 |
| Nadya Fouad | Educational Psychology | 2008 |
| Carolyn Aita | Chemistry/Biochemistry | 2011 |
| Margo Anderson | History/Urban Studies | 2013 |
| Fatemeh Zahedi | Business | 2016 |
| Christine Kovach | Nursing | 2017 |
| Kathleen Dolan | Political Science | 2017 |
| Trudy Turner | Anthropology | 2018 |
| Karyn Frick | Psychology | 2021 |

*Professor Emerita Ferne Yangyeitie Caulker-Bronson with dance students, 2015.*

a pioneer in nursing informatics and a strong advocate for nursing research.

Norma Lang, a specialist in quality assurance, outcome measures, and public policy, was appointed dean in 1980 and continued the planning for a PhD program in nursing, which had begun under Mary Conway, dean from 1976 to 1980. The doctoral program was approved in 1984, and in 2003, the now College of Nursing again led the way in advanced training, by establishing, under Dean Sally Lundeen, the first asynchronous online nursing PhD in the world.

Women faculty were also prominent in other fields. For example, Ferne Yangyeitie Caulker-Bronson, now professor emerita in the Department of Dance in UWM's Peck School of the Arts, founded the Ko-Thi Dance Company, one of the first African dance companies in the country, in Milwaukee in 1969. She taught at UWM from 1971 to 2016, cementing its reputation as a leader in teaching and performing African dance. Caulker-Bronson was also an activist in the long fight for racial equality, social justice, and fair housing in Milwaukee. Leading faculty also included Professor of Anthropology Nancy Lurie, a world-renowned specialist in Native American history and culture who became the chair of the Department of Anthropology in 1963, and Distinguished Professor of Sociology Joan Moore, a specialist on crime and gangs, who shaped the Department of Sociology

from 1975 to 1995 and was one of the main architects of the Urban Studies graduate program.

Throughout the 1970s and into the 1980s, campuses were required to report on their compliance with the provisions of Title IX and with those of other laws and executive orders regarding discrimination. A series of campus and UW System task forces on the status of women carried out evaluations. The major findings of these task forces were quite bleak: women were still clustered in lower status and low-paying positions, sexual harassment and campus security remained serious issues, and policies regarding equal opportunity had not had much impact. Furthermore, there had been little change in the percentages of tenured women faculty since 1970, even though by 1982 the percentage of women assistant professors at UWM had gone up significantly, to 43 percent, much higher than that of the UW System as a whole, where the percentage was 28.4. At every faculty rank and among academic staff, women's salaries were less than men's by anywhere from 7 to 12 percent. The task forces made a number of recommendations for improvements, but how these were to be monitored and implemented was not specified.

The mid-1980s saw a period of backlash and retrenchment, from the national to the campus level, which also led to renewed activism. When in 1983 the Reagan administration proposed a zero budget for enforcement of the 1974 Women's Educational Equity Act, both the Wisconsin Women's Council and the Wisconsin Women's Network, including members from UWM, worked for changes to state statutes that would prohibit discrimination on the basis of sex, race, religion, disability, or national origin. At UWM, Student Association leaders excluded the Women's Caucus from their 1986–1987 budget. They also did not fund the Women's Transit Service, claiming that there was low ridership and poor management. Students, staff, and faculty immediately formed Friends of Women's Transit in protest, and the ride service continued.

Even as the number of women faculty inched up in the 1980s, they remained concentrated in certain schools and colleges. There were no tenured women in what was then the School of Business Administration, only one each in what was then the School of Library Science and the College of Engineering & Applied Science, and only two in the School of Architecture & Urban Planning. This was despite healthy enrollment by women students in many of these programs. In 1989, for

example, 43 percent of students in the School of Business Administration were women, including 40 percent of the master's students and 35 percent of the PhD students.

Complaints of both gender and racial bias in tenure considerations were filed in several cases in the late 1980s and early 1990s; the highest profile case was that of Ceil Pillsbury, an assistant professor of accounting in the School of Business Administration. The case was taken up by both local and national media—including Ed Bradley's CBS television show *Street Stories*—as both the allegations of harassment and bad behavior were too juicy to remain simply a campus matter. (Attempting to portray Pillsbury as flirtatious, male colleagues reported that she had worn an allegedly "sexy" sweater, featuring stockings dangling from her breasts, to a Christmas party; the sweater was actually high necked, made of chunky yarn, and depicted several stockings over a fireplace.)

The Pillsbury case, along with other lawsuits and complaints involving sexual discrimination and harassment, or violations of equal opportunity policies for women and minority faculty, led to several investigations at UWM. The Wisconsin Joint Legislative Audit Bureau and the US Department of Labor's Office of Federal Contract Compliance Programs (OFCCP) both carried out investigations, unearthing a host of problems. OFCCP's scathing Notice of Violations, issued October 28, 1992, found

*Ceil Pillsbury teaching in what was then the School of Business Administration, 1996.* Photo courtesy Bill Herrick.

▼

evidence of sexual harassment, and that "UWM has discriminated against women by allowing such harassment and creating or tolerating a hostile working environment." It also found a "pattern and practice of discrimination" against women and minority faculty. In response, UWM entered into a conciliation agreement that would be in force for the next several years.

The Labor Department's findings were not news to most women faculty and staff. Ceil Pillsbury had been denied tenure in 1989, and within two years women faculty across campus responded by forming the Women Faculty Caucus, an ad hoc group that sought to provide better support for junior women and bring about other changes. Somewhat later, a group of women faculty and administrators formed a chapter of Wisconsin Women in Higher Education Leadership to increase both the number and effectiveness of women in leadership positions. At the UW System level, the administrators of the Women's Studies and Ethnic Studies programs jointly created the Outstanding Women of Color in Education Award in 1994 to honor women of color nominated by each UW campus for their leadership in advancing diversity and equity. UWM's first awardee was Diane S. Pollard, a faculty member in educational psychology, for her work on race and gender in education. To date, twenty-six other UWM women have received this award for a wide variety of contributions. They include Kimberly M. Blaeser, for her poetry and for founding the Milwaukee Native American Literary Cooperative; M. Estrella Sotomayor, for her innovative teaching in Spanish, including the creation of special courses for health professionals; Chia Youyee Vang, for her scholarship on the Hmong diaspora and creation of the interdisciplinary Hmong Diaspora Studies Certificate program; and Vice-Chancellor for Global Inclusion & Engagement (and multiple-degree alumna) Joan M. Prince, for her leadership on campus projects and community engagement.

Women's Studies held a day-long workshop in 1992, "Breaking the Glass Ceiling in Higher Education," attended by nearly one hundred people. It led to the creation of the Task Force on Gender Equity chaired by Merry Wiesner-Hanks, director of Women's Studies from 1992 to 1996 and 2001 to 2005. Both the workshop and the task force made a number of recommendations about

### Outstanding Women of Color in Education Award Recipients:

| | |
|---|---|
| Diane S. Pollard | 1995 |
| Twyla McGhee | 1996 |
| Diane Amour | 1997 |
| Sandra Million Underwood | 1998 |
| Karma S. Rogers | 1998 |
| Liliana Amporo | 1998 |
| April Holland | 1999 |
| Pauli Taylorboyd | 2000 |
| Cheryl S. Ajirotutu | 2001 |
| Judith Rozie-Battle | 2002 |
| Gwat-Yong Lie | 2002 |
| Joyce F. Kirk | 2003 |
| Pamela Clark | 2004/2005 |
| Alice Jackson | 2006 |
| Portia Cobb | 2007 |
| Linda Huang | 2008 |
| Kathy Berry | 2009 |
| Christine Lowery | 2010 |
| M. Estrella Sotomayor | 2011 |
| Kimberly M. Blaeser | 2012 |
| Angela Lang | 2012 |
| Sharon Adams | 2013 |
| Chia Youyee Vang | 2014 |
| Michelle Lopez-Rios | 2015 |
| Brenda Cárdenas | 2018 |
| Joan M. Prince | 2019 |
| Doris Johnson Browne | 2021 |

mentoring, childcare, safety, campus climate on diversity issues, pay equity, and parental leave. The most immediate result was the creation of a mentoring program for junior faculty women—soon expanded to include men—directed by Nadya Fouad, professor of educational psychology, whose research expertise included career development. By 1998, more than two hundred people were involved, working in mentor/mentee pairs. According to Paula M. Rhyner, the program's second coordinator, the numbers stayed strong during the early 2000s; however, current director John Reisel puts participation today at about fifty, in part because there have been so few new faculty hires.

The early 1990s also saw a renewal of student activism around women's issues. The Student

Association, and particularly Roxanne Patton, its Women's Issues chair, pushed for the opening of a women's center, a project that had wide support across campus. Carmen Witt, dean of students from 1979 to 1996 and the first woman in the UW System to hold that position, was enthusiastic. The Women's Resource Center (WRC) opened in November 1993 under the leadership of Cathy Seasholes, with a meeting room and resource library, as well as a program of speakers, targeted discussion groups, readings, performances, and events to fulfill its mission of encouraging campus awareness of women's issues, celebrating women's creativity, and providing support and advocacy. In its first ten years, according to data collected by its staff, the WRC sponsored over 450 programs and outreach activities that reached more than 60,000 people and provided employment or internships to nearly 100 students.

Women's Studies continued to grow as an academic program. By 1990, it offered more than fifty classes a year to more than two thousand students. Under directors Margo Anderson (formerly Conk), who served from 1983 to 1989, and Janice Yoder, from 1989 to 1992, the program put increasing emphasis on research, both independently and as part of the UW System's Women's and Gender Studies Consortium. In 1991, two graduate students in English—Cheryl Kader and Thomas Piontek—organized the first national graduate student conference on lesbian and gay studies, "Flaunting It,"

▲

*Opening of the UWM Women's Resource Center, 1993. Left to right: Chancellor John H. Schroeder, Dean of Students Carmen Witt, UWM Student Association President Laurie Marks, Women's Resource Center Director Cathy Seasholes, Student Association Women's Issues Director Roxanne Patton, and Director of Women's Studies Merry Wiesner-Hanks. Photo by Alan Magayne-Roshak.*

with support from Women's Studies and the Cream City Foundation. According to Kader, the conference provided the impetus for the creation of UWM's undergraduate LGBT Studies Certificate program.

In 1994, Women's Studies celebrated its twentieth anniversary with a multipart program partially sponsored by the Wisconsin Humanities Council. Entitled "Laverne and Shirley Hit the Books: Women's Studies and the Milwaukee Community," the event focused on women in education, the labor movement, and community activism. Women's Studies began the Annual UWM Student Paper and Project Contest for undergraduates and graduates, and the Annual MPS Middle and High School Essay Contest, "Wisconsin Women Making History," to which Milwaukee Public School students submitted essays about women's contributions to their communities. Women's Studies developed new courses, including Global Feminisms; launched an interdisciplinary graduate certificate in 1995; and created scholarships for low-income students whose academic careers were threatened by changes in state welfare rules.

*"Flaunting It" conference flyer, 1991.*

▼

*"Laverne and Shirley Hit the Books" program cover, 1994.*

The 1990s saw the first high-level women administrators outside of nursing. Kate Davy arrived in 1994 as dean of what was then the School of Fine Arts and carried out strong measures to promote diversity. In 1998, Nancy Zimpher became UWM's first woman chancellor, creating a strong presence in the community through an array of programs and initiatives under the umbrella heading of the Milwaukee Idea designed to connect the campus with the community. Student enrollment grew to nearly twenty-five thousand by the end of Zimpher's tenure as chancellor in 2003. Women made up 55 percent of undergraduates and more than 60 percent of graduate students.

By 2000, women made up about 36 percent of the faculty, though turnover among women

and minority faculty remained high. Responding to the rate of turnover and other issues, Zimpher commissioned a task force to examine the climate on campus for women, chaired by Fouad. The task force found many of the same problems identified twenty-five years earlier: exclusion from decision-making, discrimination and harassment, unresponsiveness to complaints, lack of accountability, and a chilly climate. Some of the recommendations made by the task force were implemented, including the establishment of a permanent Equity Council, which later became the campus Ombuds Council.

The years since 2003 have been ones of expansion and then contraction at UWM. Enrollment grew to an all-time high of more than thirty thousand students in 2010, with an increased emphasis on externally funded research. Women faculty and staff were essential parts of the growth in research, receiving major grants and awards from the National Institutes of Health, the National Science Foundation, the US Department of Education, and other funding agencies and foundations. Professor of English Anne Basting, for example, received a MacArthur Foundation Fellowship for her work bringing meaning and purpose to the lives of older adults through storytelling, poetry, and performance. There was a building boom. The library was renovated, and Ewa Barczyk was appointed director in 2007, the first woman to hold this position; she served in the post until 2016.

Some of the issues that had long been of concern to women on campus were overlooked or set aside during this boom period, however. The campus Ombuds Council lapsed, and the UW System-mandated climate survey was advertised so poorly that the response rate was too low to make the results statistically significant. Early

*2018 Milwaukee Public Schools (MPS) essay contest winners and their mothers, all Rohingya Muslim immigrants, with their teacher, Erin Sivek, from MPS's International Newcomer Center, located at the Milwaukee Academy of Chinese Language.* Photo courtesy Merry Wiesner-Hanks.

certificate. In 2002, it made its first joint appointment hire: Christina Ewig, as an assistant professor in both the Department of Political Science and Women's Studies. Several other joint appointment hires followed. Women's Studies hosted the 2004 National Women's Studies Association annual conference, which brought hundreds of scholars to Milwaukee. In 2004, it began to offer a bachelor's degree. The first master's students in Women's Studies enrolled in 2010, with two dual-degree master's programs established soon after, with the School of Information Studies and the Helen Bader School of Social Welfare. In 2012, Women's Studies hired its first full-time assistant professor, Xin Huang, who received tenure and promotion in fall 2019. Faculty with joint appointments who retired or left UWM for positions elsewhere were not replaced, however, and requests for further tenure-track appointments were turned down. Reflecting changes in the field, Women's Studies became Women's & Gender Studies (WGS) in 2014.

versions of Chancellor Carlos E. Santiago's Campus Master Plan called for the demolition of the Child Care Center to make way for a new science building, without providing for the center's relocation. Intense pressure from students, staff, and faculty who were parents, and their allies, eventually compelled the administration to find suitable space for the Child Care Center, and it was relocated.

Contraction began in 2011, when the election of officials hostile to public education in Wisconsin brought major budget cuts, the disbanding of public unions (including that for teaching assistants at UWM), and threats to the tenure system. Salaries stagnated and take-home pay shrank, and faculty and staff retired or left. The number of faculty declined from 866 in 2011 to 732 in 2020, with the share of women holding stable at about 40 percent. The number of people employed full- and part-time as academic staff, about 60 percent of whom were women, increased slightly over this period, in part as tenure-track positions were converted to lower-paid and less secure lectureships and other types of contingent positions, reflecting a national trend. The number of students dropped significantly, further decreasing the budget.

This pattern of expansion and then contraction has been shared by most academic units, including Women's Studies. In the 2000s, Women's Studies devoted much of its attention to growing its academic offerings and consolidating its visibility on and off campus. Throughout the decade it created new undergraduate courses, including Queer Theory, which became a requirement for the LGBT Studies

Women's & Gender Studies has continued to cosponsor numerous events with student organizations, centers, and departments. Thanks to the generosity of Kumkum Sangari, William F. Vilas Research Professor of English and the Humanities, it has offered an annual Feminist Lecture Series since 2007. In 2014, WGS celebrated its fortieth anniversary with an undergraduate poster exhibition and a lecture by Women's Studies alumna Astrid Henry, the Louise R. Noun Chair of Women's Studies at Grinnell College.

Women's activism on core issues persisted. In 2010, Kate Kramer, deputy director of UWM's Center for 21st Century Studies; Stacey Oliker, associate professor of sociology; and Amanda Seligman, associate professor of history—

*Women's Resource Center staff, 2011.*
Photo courtesy Cathy Seasholes.

members of the Provost's Task Force on Family Leave—carried out a comprehensive study to which over eleven hundred employees responded. They prepared a report on UWM's policy and practice that recommended changes at multiple levels, from the UW System through individual departments; some of these were implemented, and some were not. At a campus-wide diversity and climate event in 2011, Women's Studies Assistant Director Kathy Miller-Dillon and Gwynne Kennedy, director from 2006 to 2013 and chair from 2018 to 2019, returned to the report of the 2001 Task Force on the Climate for Women to review UWM's efforts to implement its recommendations. Few of them had been put into effect. In response, over thirty women faculty and staff created their own ad hoc women's issues working group, thus repeating what women had done in founding CSAW forty years earlier. The group could not sustain itself for very long, however, because of the heavy workloads and other obligations of its members, and the scope of the challenges needing to be addressed.

Over the last twenty years, the Women's Resource Center has continued to sponsor workshops, conferences, service projects, art exhibits, concerts, donation drives, and other events and services, often in collaboration with campus and community partners. Since 2018, it has sponsored the Black Feminist Symposium, which brings together students, faculty, staff, and community members to share their research, experiences, and creative work to foster a much-needed space for Black-identified women to feel connected to other women. Recognizing the need to support student-parents, the WRC works closely with the Life Impact Program to do what it can to assist them; in the words of WRC Assistant Director Justice Johnson, a Life Impact alum, "What the WRC can do to help the program, it will do."

Since 2016, Panthers Against Sexual Assault, founded by Nataley Neuman, has been the most active student feminist group on campus, educating about sexual assault, advocating for survivors, and presenting information about resources. With the WRC, it has organized Take Back the Night rallies and events for Sexual Assault Awareness Month every March.

The year 2021 marks half a century since women students, staff, and faculty formed the first groups advocating for a wide range of issues of concern for women on campus. On some issues, there has been decided progress. Well over half of the students enrolled in bachelor's and PhD programs are women, and nearly two-thirds of those enrolled in master's programs; among some ethnic groups the proportion of women students is even higher. Women faculty form twice as large a share of the faculty (42 percent) as they did in 1971 (20 percent). There is a solid program in Women's & Gender Studies offering an undergraduate major and minor, master's degree, and graduate certificate; a Women's Resource

▲

*Nataley Neuman, winner of the 2018 Casey O'Brien*
*Outstanding Activist Award, with Casey O'Brien.*
Photo courtesy Merry Wiesner-Hanks.

Center providing services for students; a day care
center; and a faculty mentoring program. All of
these exist today because of thousands of hours
of meetings, organizing, direct actions, proposal
drafting, lobbying, participation on campus
committees, mentoring and networking, and
educating others carried out by many hundreds of
individuals over the decades. Many of these gains
are fragile, however, as centers, programs, and
offices devoted to women's issues remain severely
underresourced or transitory. As has been widely
reported, Covid-19 has had a disproportionate
impact on women, including students, faculty,
and staff at UWM, and it will be important moving
forward to recognize this and to put extra effort
toward creating the equitable and welcoming
campus envisioned over the decades by so
many women.

Authors' note: The stories we heard and uncovered
while we were writing this chapter inspired us to
write a longer and more detailed version of this
history, which can be found at:
https://dc.uwm.edu/uwmhistory/.

CHAPTER

# 6

# Building Community Connectedness: LGBTQ+ History at UWM

MICHAEL DOYLEN AND
JENNIFER (JEN) MURRAY

*University of Wisconsin-Milwaukee (UWM) undergraduate students Farok Rashid (left) and Audrey DeGuzman participating in a pride celebration in downtown Milwaukee, 2018.* Photo by Elora Hennessey.

The history of LGBTQ+ communities at the University of Wisconsin-Milwaukee (UWM) mirrors the history of those communities within the broader culture. It is a story that moves from student-led efforts to organize and achieve visibility in the 1970s, to uneven institutional recognition in the 1980s and 1990s, to bolder engagement by the university with issues of intersectional identities in the 2000s. Throughout the decades, the terminology used to describe LGBTQ+ people has continued to change and evolve, and the authors have tried to use the terms that were current at the time, rather than impose contemporary language on those who came before us.

The authors present this chapter as an institutional history of LGBTQ+ communities at UWM. It is focused on the development of student organizations and student services, academic programs, policy reform, and faculty/staff organizing. Absent are stories of individual students, faculty, and staff that would bring more texture and color to this history. The existing source material, which supports deep research into administrative matters, has less to say, for example, about the personal experiences of students coming out in the 1970s or faculty gender transitioning mid career. We acknowledge the limitations of this work and hope the chapter provides context and inspiration for other histories.

UWM has been home to LGBTQ+ student organizations for more than fifty years. These groups provided LGBTQ+ students with a sense of belonging and an opportunity to develop a positive sense of self in a supportive environment. They also benefitted the wider campus by calling attention to issues of importance to LGBTQ+ communities and their allies. Finally, student groups frequently served as a force for change to improve the campus climate and make UWM a more welcoming place for all.

Established in 1970, the Gay Liberation Organization (GLO) was the first gay and lesbian student organization to be officially chartered at UWM. (The Homosexual Freedom League predated GLO by two months, but it was never chartered.)

*Cover of the manifesto of the Gay Liberation Organization (GLO), circa 1970. GLO was the first gay and lesbian student group officially chartered at UWM.*

GLO's goals included repealing Wisconsin's so-called "sexual perversion" law, which had been in place since 1836, and educating the mainstream community about gay culture. Although the *UWM Post* published largely supportive articles and letters about GLO, Chancellor J. Martin Klotsche received numerous complaints about budding gay organizations. One outraged citizen asked if there were "limits of any kind at UWM" and another implored Klotsche to "restore some decency and respect to our fine university." In response, campus administration affirmed the rights of gay and lesbian students to organize like other students but stopped short of further support.

The first meeting of GLO, in March, attracted about seventy-five people. From the very beginning, GLO appeared split between members who supported social change through education and legislative reform and those who espoused the revolutionary goals of gay liberation. GLO members also debated whether to pursue civil rights for gays and lesbians exclusively or to form coalitions with other oppressed minority groups. Such tensions were common across organizations of this time. In fact, many split along ideological lines into either assimilationist organizations centered around white, gender-conforming individuals who wanted to enjoy the full privileges of the straight, white middle class, or into radical, intersectional organizations seeking fundamental social changes.

Within a few months, tensions between the moderate and radical elements of GLO had increased. In May, those who were more militant likely participated in a campus demonstration that drew an estimated three thousand protestors. They included members of Students for a Democratic Society, faculty, union leaders, and activists opposing—among other things—US involvement in Vietnam and Cambodia and the shooting at Kent State University. The protest shut down portions of UWM and prompted Klotsche to declare a state of emergency. Soon after, GLO's more radical members left the group and reorganized as the community-based Milwaukee Gay Liberation Front (GLF).

Leaving revolutionary politics to Milwaukee GLF, GLO adopted a more moderate agenda. When it registered as a student organization in February 1971, it renamed itself the Gay People's Union at UWM (GPU) with the aim of providing "a dignified social and cultural climate for Gay students at UWM." Indeed, at the first meeting of the group under its new name, according to university records, members made a point of focusing on "realistic gay activism." Over the following months, GPU organized film screenings, a dance open to the public, and a few parties. In September 1971, however, GPU ended its short life as a student organization and became a community organization that went on to have lasting impact on Milwaukee's emerging LGBTQ+ communities. Following the demise of GPU on campus, students formed the Gay Students Association (GSA) "to make gays aware that gay is good and to educate straight people to the realities of gay life." Like its predecessor, GSA was active only briefly, from spring 1974 to spring 1975.

A new organization named the Gay Community at UWM emerged in fall 1975 and lasted a remarkable twenty-three years. It organized the first Gay Day at UWM, held on

PH: 963-6555
Gay Community at UWM

COMING OUT
A DISCUSSION IN 2 PARTS
PT. 1 - mar. 12th  union e 309
PT. 2 - mar. 19th  union e 307
4:30 pm.

THE UNIVERSITY OF WISCONSIN-MILWAUKEE  UNION BOX 251  MILWAUKEE, WI 53201
...SERVICE  ...SUPPORT  ...FRIENDSHIP

*Flyer for an event sponsored by the Gay Community at UWM, 1980. The group, organized in 1975, changed its name numerous times over its twenty-three-year-long history.*

April 23, 1980, to increase visibility and promote discussion of social and political issues. Its leaders encouraged people to demonstrate solidarity by wearing blue jeans, and its members put up posters and set up an informational booth in the concourse of the Student Union. Unfortunately, some students heckled the event organizers, pelted them with eggs, and threatened to bomb the Gay Community office. Although Gay Day celebrations in 1981 and 1982 were met with less disruption—due mostly to the increased presence of campus police and private security hired by organizers—one event was cancelled in 1982 because of what was described as a "hostile atmosphere."

Over time, the organization repeatedly changed its name to better reflect the growing diversity of its members. By spring 1985, for example, the group was known as the Gay and Lesbian Community at UWM, organizing Gay and Lesbian Awareness Week on a semiregular basis into the early 1990s. (From spring 1988 to spring 1990, the group became the Ten Percent Society—a reference to the findings of Alfred Kinsey that ten percent of the male population is homosexual—and organized events around National Coming Out Day.) In fall 1992, the group changed its name again, to the Gay, Lesbian, Bisexual Community at UWM; in February 1996, it sponsored a Lesbian/Gay/Bisexual Awareness Week. Two years later, it became the Rainbow Alliance, explicitly including transgender people in its statement of purpose. It continued to exist until 2005, featuring guest speakers, workshops, entertainment, and socializing.

At times, other LGBTQ+ student organizations existed at UWM, pursuing their own purposes and agendas. United Gay Students at UWM, for example, worked from spring 1980 to fall 1984 to secure legal rights for gay men and lesbians. Lavender Commitment was created in December 1981 to promote gay and lesbian arts and culture at UWM, organizing annual gay and lesbian film festivals at the UWM Union Cinema from 1983 to 1989 and later sponsoring the Milwaukee LGBT Film/Video Festival. UWM's chapter of Delta Lambda Phi, an international social fraternity for gay men and their allies, was active from 1993 through 1996.

In the 2000s, the number and level of activity of LGBTQ+ student organizations declined due to the existence of the LGBTQ+ Resource Center, which since its opening in 2002 has provided the connect on and support that many students previously found in student organizations. Although student groups continue to form, they are organized around specific segments of the student population and tend to be short lived. Notable organizations that emerged in the 2000s included Queer People of Color, the first group formed to address the unique needs of queer students of color, in fall 2008; a local chapter of Out in Science, Technology, Engineering, and Mathematics Inc., a professional association for LGBTQ+ individuals in the STEM community, in fall 2011; Faith N Queers, a group supporting students exploring the intersections of LGBTQ+ identities and spirituality, in fall 2011; and Pulse, the first LGBTQ+ organization for graduate students, in 2017.

In addition to promoting pride and educating those on campus about issues important to LGBTQ+ people, student organizations worked to reform UWM policies to make the campus a more welcoming place for everyone. For example, the Gay Community partnered with academic staff and faculty governance in the late 1970s to include the term "sexual preference" in the university's nondiscrimination policy. The first public statement on the policy appeared in an open letter from Chancellor Werner A. Baum to the campus published in the *UWM Post* on August 28, 1978. Further efforts led to even wider impact. In 1982, for example, student activist Leon Rouse played a key role in the passage of Wisconsin's historic law—the first in the nation—banning discrimination based on sexuality in employment, housing, and public accommodations.

In the 1930s, colleges and universities across the country began to grapple with questions of discrimination raised by the presence of Reserve Officer Training Corps (ROTC) programs on their campuses. At the time, the Department of Defense considered homosexuality incompatible with military service and grounds for discharge. Gay and lesbian students could enroll in military science classes offered by college-based military training programs such as ROTC, but they were ineligible for admission to the programs. In 1982, Rouse and fellow activist Eric Enberg protested such policies,

Thomas Piontek and attended by more than three hundred students from North America and Canada.

In fall 1992, a group of employees formed the UWM LGB Faculty/Staff Caucus to address campus climate, expand coverage of gay and lesbian issues in the curriculum, and extend spousal benefits to same-sex couples. Jeffrey Merrick, at the time an associate professor of history, served as the first coordinator. The caucus worked with the Gay, Lesbian, Bisexual Community at UWM and participated in meetings of the recently formed University of Wisconsin System's LGB Issues Network. The caucus continued to exist into the 2000s.

In July 1993, Dean of Students Carmen Witt named Thomas Dake, student services program manager in the Office of Student Life, to the office's newly created position of liaison for lesbian, gay, and bisexual students. And in another nod to the Kinsey studies from the 1940s, Witt funded the position at four hours per week, the equivalent of 10 percent of the number of hours worked by a full-time employee. As liaison, Dake served as a point of contact between students and various units of the university and as a consultant to campus administration on matters of sexual orientation. Dake coordinated UWM's Safe Space program, which distributed magnets featuring the Safe Space symbol (a pink triangle in a green circle) to faculty and staff as a way for them to signal their support for LGB students. He also coordinated various events and programs, including an ambitious LGB Speaker Series during the 1994 and 1995 academic years.

At the urging of the LGB Faculty/Staff Caucus, UWM Chancellor John H. Schroeder charged a task force in summer 1993 to investigate and make recommendations concerning issues of importance to LGB communities at UWM. The Task Force on Lesbian, Gay, and Bisexual Issues presented its report in December 1994, concluding that despite the significant changes in law and institutional policy that had occurred over the past two decades, UWM still had work to do to create a welcoming and accepting climate

noting they violated UWM's policy prohibiting discrimination based on sexual preference. In April 1985, the UWM Faculty Senate voted to remove the ROTC program unless it amended its policies, but then reversed itself when a group of faculty members who disagreed with that decision gained enough support to have the matter reconsidered. On September 19, 1985, UWM faculty voted 157 to 111 to keep the program on campus. There the matter rested until President Barack Obama signed into law the Don't Ask, Don't Tell Repeal Act in December 2010, allowing gay men, lesbians, and bisexuals to serve openly in the US military without fear of reprisal.

The 1990s opened with a significant first as UWM hosted "Flaunting It: The First National Graduate Student Conference on Lesbian and Gay Studies" on April 18, 1991. The conference was organized by graduate students Cheryl Kader and for LGB students and employees. It noted, for example, that LGB students reported incidents of insensitivity, harassment, and physical threats or confrontation. The report went on to call for continued assessment of the campus climate for LGB students and employees, sensitivity training for administrators and employees working in student services, and workshops on sexual orientation and homophobia for faculty and staff. It also recommended creating a certificate program in the emerging field of gay and lesbian studies and urged support for legislative efforts to extend domestic partner benefits to employees.

Yet, by the time the report of the Task Force on LGB Issues reached Schroeder's desk, significant progress had already been made when it came to increasing the coverage of LGB issues in the curriculum. The College of Letters and Science faculty, for example, had approved a proposal for a gay and lesbian studies certificate program in December 1993. Final approval, which also required UW System authorization, was put on hold due to a freeze on new academic programs ordered by UW System President Katharine Lyall pending authorization of the 1995–1997 biennial budget.

In the meantime, the proposal attracted the attention of the local media with the story breaking in the *Milwaukee Journal* and *Milwaukee Sentinel* in late February 1994. A conservative radio talk show host opined that the program amounted to "group therapy" for a special interest group, and the university's plans drew swift opposition from state legislators. State Representatives Bonnie Ladwig, Steve Nass, and John Dobyns circulated a letter of protest cosigned by twenty-seven of their legislative colleagues to University of Wisconsin Board of Regents President George K. Steil Sr. The legislators objected to the costs associated with the new program, questioned the legitimacy of gay and lesbian studies as a field of study, and lamented the further splintering of people into special interest groups. "Undoubtedly issues affecting a certain group of people who choose a particular type of lifestyle should not constitute an academic department," the objecting representatives wrote. Steil sidestepped the issues of academic rigor and multiculturalism, noting that the regents had no role in the approval process given that the proposal included no new funding.

*UWM Safe Space program brochure, circa 1993. The program provided a way for faculty and staff to signal support for lesbian, gay, and bisexual students.*

UWM's Gay and Lesbian Studies Certificate program, the first of its kind in the UW System, was approved in November 1995, when the Board of Regents eliminated the need for UW System authorization for new submajor or certificate programs and required only that such programs be approved at the campus level. The program was also among the earliest in the United States to be organized as an independent, interdisciplinary area of study (i.e., instead of as a track or concentration within an academic major). Christopher Lane, assistant professor of English and comparative literature, served as the first program coordinator. A description of the certificate program first appeared in the 1997–1998 *UWM Undergraduate Bulletin*. In spring 2000, its name was changed to the Lesbian, Gay, Bisexual, and Transgender Studies

Certificate program to be more inclusive and more accurately reflect the content of courses being taught.

In the years since 2000, the program, today known as LGBTQ+ Studies, grew significantly. Between 2000 and 2010, course offerings expanded from one to three per year, with typically up to three students earning the LGBT Studies Undergraduate Certificate annually. However, the program was severely underfunded and lacked a dedicated coordinator.

With the future of the program in danger, Associate Professor of Sociology Cary Gabriel Costello stepped in as its director in 2011, determined to find ways to support and grow the program. (Costello continues to direct the LGBTQ+ Studies program today.) Staff from LGBT Studies, what was then the LGBT Resource Center, the Milwaukee LGBT Film/Video Festival, and the Golda Meir Library worked together to secure two outside grants that supported a number of new activities. In 2012, Costello and the LGBT Studies Advisory Committee organized "Sex and Gender Spectra," a three-day national conference that drew hundreds of attendees. The conference addressed myriad topics related to sexuality and gender variance: intersexuality, androgyny, gender transition, the multiplicity of sexes and sexualities in world cultures, and gender policing. LGBT Studies also initiated a visiting scholar program, giving queer and trans scholars an institutional home for a year of activities. And it added additional classes, so that today LGBTQ+ Studies offers eight to nine classes per year, graduating numerous certificate students.

Another sort of progress came in the mid-1990s when the Golda Meir Library's Archives and Special Collections began actively collecting and preserving primary source material on LGBTQ+ topics to support teaching and research at UWM. Since then, the library has developed one of the largest LGBTQ+ historical collections in Wisconsin. The collection is especially important for documenting local Milwaukee history, but also includes books, magazines, and newspaper articles that tell a national story. To supplement existing primary sources, the Archives conducted both the Milwaukee Transgender Oral History Project in 2011 and the Wisconsin HIV/AIDS History Project in 2017–2018.

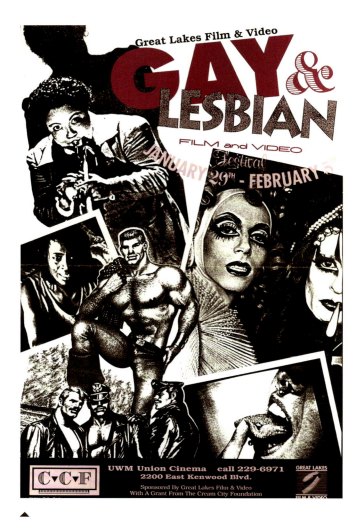

A poster promoting the 1993 Milwaukee Gay and Lesbian Film and Video Festival. UWM began hosting the festival in 1997.

In October 1997, the Department of Film in what was then the School of Fine Arts began hosting the Milwaukee Gay and Lesbian Film and Video Festival. Great Lakes Film & Video, a non-profit organization that promoted the production and exhibition of local and regional media arts, had managed this highly popular, local film festival from 1992 to 1996, handing the operation of the festival over to UWM when it faced staff turnover and financial issues. Under the direction of Carl Bogner, today a senior lecturer in film, video, animation, and new genres at today's Peck School of the Arts, the festival became a regular highlight of the Milwaukee LGBTQ+ social season, featuring an entertaining and edifying mix of coming out films, romantic comedies, documentaries, and shorts reflecting the diversity of its audience. In 2000, the Milwaukee LGBT Film/Video Festival began holding its opening night screening at the Oriental Theatre, Milwaukee's historic movie palace.

UWM LGBT Resource Center, 2016. Established in 2002 and now the LGBTQ+ Resource Center, it offers workshops and training on issues important to UWM's LGBTQ+ community.

The festival ended in 2019, after a remarkable thirty-four-year-long run.

In the early 2000s, students began pressing for establishment of an LGBT resource center, with the Segregated University Fee Allocation Committee making a proposal to the UWM Student Association that highlighted the importance of and need for such a move. The proposal had numerous supporters, including the Rainbow Alliance, student groups, campus administrators, and local organizations. The Student Association approved the proposal in December 2000, and authorized funding for a full-time director and student employees. The UWM LGBT Resource Center celebrated its grand opening on September 25, 2002, with a presentation by Cuban American writer, translator, and activist Achy Obejas; a ribbon-cutting ceremony the following day; and extensive programming during Coming Out Week the following month. The center is now known as the LGBTQ+ Resource Center.

Since its launch, the Resource Center has offered robust educational workshops and training for students, faculty, and staff. Especially noteworthy is the center's program in LGBTQ+ Intersectionality Focused Training, which offers both presentations and workshops on a variety of topics designed to raise awareness of issues of importance to UWM's LGBTQ+ communities, and

approximately twenty training programs annually. In 2017, in collaboration with UWM's Inclusive Excellence Center and its Center for Excellence in Teaching and Learning, the Resource Center implemented a five-week LGBTQ+ inclusivity workshop and certificate program.

The Resource Center has a rich history of LGBTQ+ programming featuring prominent speakers including Keith Boykin, Margaret Cho, Tony Kushner, and Dan Savage. In 2012, the center celebrated its tenth anniversary in conjunction with the center's Fall Welcome Meet & Greet reception featuring a display created by the Golda Meir Library. And on April 24, 2013, it hosted the first-ever LGBTQ+ graduate student symposium in collaboration with the UWM Graduate School. According to organizers, it featured poster presentations by graduate students doing interdisciplinary research and a keynote address by Costello.

Although small, student-led and student-inspired programming is the primary staple of the work of the Resource Center; it has also produced a handful of signature, large-scale, annual events. These include the Drag Show, held annually since its creation by the Rainbow Alliance in 2001. Early shows were held in the Student Union's Wisconsin

▲

*Performer at UWM's annual Drag Show, 2020. Now sponsored by the LGBTQ+ Resource Center, the event was held for the first time in 2001.*

Room—and later, its Ballroom— and were attended by hundreds of students and community members. By 2015, the Drag Show had outgrown its campus venue—it was drawing audiences of close to one thousand—and found a new home on the stage of what was then the Milwaukee Theatre. It typically has served as the Resource Center's most anticipated and biggest annual event.

The Resource Center also organized the first annual Lavender Graduation at UWM in 2010. The event celebrated the achievements and identities of sixteen graduates and featured Professor Emeritus Jeffrey Merrick as the keynote speaker. UWM's LGBT+ Alumni Chapter, also established in 2010, cosponsored the event. More than 250 UWM graduates have been recognized at Lavender Graduation over the past eleven years.

The Resource Center has been at the forefront of promoting the use of both preferred name and inclusive pronouns at UWM. To this end, in 2011, it developed an informational card listing eight different pronouns—some traditional, others not— and illustrating pronoun usage depending on where a pronoun is placed in a sentence. The card not only helped demystify the use of nontraditional pronouns, but also embraced the diversity of nonbinary gender identities. Featured in news stories by the BBC and the *New York Times*, the card was widely distributed and used across the United States.

Along with the Resource Center, the Chancellor's Advisory Committee for LGBTQ+ Advocacy has been a consistent force for positive change at UWM. Established by Schroeder in 1995 as the Advisory Committee on Lesbian, Gay, and Bisexual Issues, the committee works to improve climate and diversity by making recommendations related to current and proposed policies affecting LGBTQ+ students and employees.

In February 2005, the Resource Center and the Chancellor's Advisory Committee jointly proposed a visible and accessible gender-neutral restroom in the Student Union. The recommendation aligned with national movements that support safe alternatives to multi-stall, gender-specific restrooms, which can be problematic for transgender, gender-nonconforming, and other individuals. Costello, who served on the committee, recalled initial pushback from the Union Policy Board, the Physical Environment Committee, and several individual stakeholders. Claims centered around the belief that cis women would somehow be put at risk, that the expense of benefitting a tiny group of individuals was prohibitive, and that the move might draw negative attention from the state legislature. The Resource Center and Chancellor's Advisory Committee redoubled their efforts, forming alliances with other stakeholders including the Student Association, the Americans with Disabilities Act Advisory Committee, and the Life Impact Program. The inclusive facilities policy was eventually adopted in September 2014.

This policy, which has been reviewed and updated over the years, continues to be used in campus planning for preexisting and new campus building renovations. During 2019–2020, a working group of the City of Milwaukee Equal Rights Commission, with input from Jennifer (Jen) Murray—at the time the director of the LGBTQ+ Resource Center—wrote a resolution on inclusive restroom facilities in city-owned properties that referenced UWM policy.

The Chancellor's Advisory Committee has been instrumental in effecting other changes at UWM. In May 2017, the committee made recommendations to the Institutional Review Board pertaining to gender and sexuality categories in research projects and worked with other UWM partners to encourage the listing of pronouns in the UWM syllabus policy. Since 2016, the committee has administered the LGBTQ+ Champion of the Year Award, which recognizes UWM faculty and staff who have raised awareness of issues that affect LGBTQ+ individuals or proposed policies to improve climate and diversity at UWM. Past recipients of the award include Costello; Kari Dawson, assistant director, University Housing; Gary Hollander, adjunct professor of psychology and founder and former president of Diverse & Resilient, a statewide nonprofit organization supporting lesbian, gay, bisexual, transgender, and queer people; and Melissa Monier, interim assistant director of the Women's Resource Center.

Other moves also targeted inclusivity. In 2013, thanks to a policy approved by the Student Housing Administrative Council and the Student Association—both student government bodies—and the UW Board of Regents, UWM became the first school in the UW System to adopt a gender inclusive housing policy. The policy provides students with welcoming living and working environments regardless of their gender identity. Additionally, UWM has hosted regional programs such as the 2012 "Safe Schools, Safe  Communities:

State Superintendent's Conference on LGBT Youth" and the 2016 "Wisconsin Trans and Queer People of Color Summit" in 2016.

In June 2015, UWM implemented a policy that allows students to be recognized by their preferred name on most internal campus records and applications. In September 2019, the Panther Card Office began offering double-sided IDs for individuals interested in listing a preferred name/name in use on one side of the identification card and a legal name on the other.

UWM's progress in improving campus climate has been recognized in several ways. Due to the work of the Resource Center staff, the university was featured in the 2006 edition of the *College Advocate Guide for LGBT Students* for its LGBTQ+ affirming policies. In 2011, UWM was ranked twelfth among the top twenty-five Gay Friendly Campuses, according to a survey conducted by the Newsweek Daily Beast Company. The annual Campus Pride Index routinely places UWM among its top LGBTQ+ friendly colleges and universities.

UWM continues to strive to meet the needs of its LGBTQ+ communities, whose members exhibit a sustained commitment to and deep understanding of the importance of inclusive policies and practices enhancing the overall student experience and campus climate. To that end, the university is intentionally building upon the historical foundation of LGBTQ+ visibility efforts to support and uplift the advocacy and engagement of students who hold multiply marginalized and minoritized identities. As evidenced by the fifty-some years of challenges, growth, creativity, and determination that people have invested in the LGBTQ+ communities on the UWM campus, one can only trust that it will continue.

CHAPTER **7**

# Rectifying the Past, Planning the Future: Bridging Disability Awareness and Accessibility

JONATHAN BROSKOWSKI,
CHRISTI CRAIG, AND
ROGER O. SMITH

*Pet therapy event, part of Fall Welcome activities at the University of Wisconsin-Milwaukee (UWM), 2018.*

When discussions about diversity and the positive impacts of inclusivity emerge in academia, the concept of disability is often left out of the conversation. For years, researchers, politicians, and professionals have focused on finding so-called "cures" or ways to "fix" people so they might better blend into the society and culture of the majority. However, as Leyton Schnellert et al. write in *Disability Studies Quarterly*, "When viewed as a cultural concept with political/relational considerations, disability has broad-reaching impacts that can provide, according to Simi Linton, 'a prism through which one can gain a broader understanding of society and human experience.'"

Viewing disability in this light has taken time to develop roots in academia; however, topics surrounding students who have disabilities have long been a source of conversation at the University of Wisconsin-Milwaukee (UWM). Although UWM often led in the State of Wisconsin when it came to improving physical access for students with disabilities, running disability research projects, and providing accessible programs and learning experiences related to disabilities, the road to success has been rocky. Full physical and academic accessibility on campus continues to be a challenge to this day, one requiring constant vigilance and ongoing commitment. Proper accommodation and accessibility have always involved input from administration, faculty, and disability services on campus; critical to this success has been listening to and understanding the needs of students with disabilities.

The history of disability-related programming on what today is the UWM campus can be traced back to the historic Milwaukee Downer College red brick buildings. There, according to Jacqueline L. Jones, writing in the *American Journal of Occupational Therapy*, Elizabeth Greene Upham Davis in 1918 created one of the first courses of study in occupational therapy in the country, with students pursuing bachelor's degrees in other disciplines able to earn a diploma in occupational therapy. Jones noted that Davis—who hailed from a prominent Milwaukee family—worked with the Junior League of Milwaukee to found the Curative Workshop, which provided services and trained students in the new profession of occupational therapy. UWM's Greene Hall is named after Davis, with the name "Elizabeth Greene" carved in the mantel of the building's main fireplace. Furthermore, it was Greene's connection to campus that later encouraged the donation, acquisition,

◀ *A cartoon from the May 4, 1978,* UWM Post *depicting students with disabilities trying to navigate the UWM campus.*

and curation of the multimedia Curative Care Network Records collection now housed at UWM's Golda Meir Library.

Over the years, UWM has increasingly provided disability-specific professional training, today graduating professionals in physical therapy, occupational therapy, therapeutic recreation, speech-language pathology, interpreter training, special education, assistive technology, and biomedical engineering. These disability-related instructional programs, in turn, brought faculty with outstanding research pedigrees to campus to teach and to generate major lines of discovery. They also stimulated national and international recognition of UWM research and development activities, bringing the university the enviable status that comes with a strong national reputation and competitive national rankings.

As the study of disabilities took hold on campus, the number of enrolled students with disabilities increased, creating another avenue for UWM to take the lead in programming and service. Throughout its history, for example, UWM's Accessibility Resource Center (ARC) has offered more than just basic support of physical and academic access for students, establishing programs, student organizations, and partnerships across campus that would enhance the college experience for students with disabilities. These programs and services increased in size and scope as more successful accommodations in technology became available.

Five years before the Rehabilitation Act of 1973 was passed by the US Congress, Ernest Spaights recognized the importance of providing

*The name of Elizabeth Greene Upham Davis, who created one of the first courses of study in occupational therapy in the country, is carved into the mantel of this fireplace in Greene Hall at UWM, 2021.* Photo by Roger O. Smith.

minority students with equal opportunities. He cofounded the Experimental Program in Higher Education (EPHE), which focused on underrepresented students facing economic and academic challenges. Attention to this program likely sparked discussions that paved the way for both an expanded definition of the term "disadvantaged" and better access to education for other minority populations.

During his tenure as assistant chancellor in the Division of Student Affairs, Spaights also established the Advisory Committee for Handicapped Students, later the Advisory Committee for Disabled Students. This committee created a handbook of services for students who at the time were described as "handicapped," and an inventory booklet, entitled *Barriers*, that listed physical obstacles to accessibility on campus. *Barriers* became an essential resource for students navigating university grounds and for Office of Planning and Development staff with respect to building

*Ernest Spaights enters Chapman Hall, 1970. Spaights's work with the Experimental Program in Higher Education likely paved the way for increased access to education for students with disabilities.*

renovations. The committee also worked with two volunteer programs: Volunteer Services Unlimited (VSU) and Visually Impaired Student Service (VISS). According to the *UWM Post*, VSU assisted physically disabled students in moving across campus, among other things, and VISS provided resources that included magnifying machines, braille dictionaries, and cassette recordings of textbooks and volunteers to read them aloud.

In May 1972, the Advisory Committee proposed the establishment of a clearinghouse for students with disabilities. Once up and running, the new Student Information Center (SIC) became a one-stop shop for students new to campus and university life, offering services such as alternative testing and tutoring for those who needed these accommodations.

Consider, for example, the work of Professor of Art Jack Waldheim, who in 1976 developed a cassette-map navigation system for blind students. He worked with several blind students, walking the ninety-acre campus, recording landmarks, and writing a script to be paired with a textured map of campus. General Electric Medical Systems Division of Milwaukee underwrote the production of a master tape and provided cassettes for twenty-seven students. Although such projects marked the beginning of the effort to expand accessibility and accommodations on campus, architectural barriers,

▲

UWM students Kathleen Goetsch (right) and Howard Kaufman, shown in this UWM Post photo, use a campus map designed for blind people to learn how to navigate buildings and sidewalks when moving around the crowded campus, 1976.

▲

Kathy Stout (left) and Bob Tratolli, shown in this 1977 UWM Post photo, ran UWM's first program for students with hearing impairments.

mobility issues, and access to textbooks were not the only challenges students with disabilities faced at UWM. Needs varied and called for a diversification of specialized services and programs.

In 1976, SIC was replaced by the Disabled Student Services Office (DSS), where VSU, VISS, and what was known at the time as the office's Hearing Program—all formerly run by volunteers—were formalized. Two UWM students, Roger Behm and Kathy Stout, played important roles in building and organizing these programs. Behm, a blind student, worked from 1977 to 1980 as head of VISS, a position for which—Behm told the *UWM Post*—he had "jumped at the chance" to apply. According to the *Post* article, Behm believed that "students should be taught to be self-sufficient, to strive for independence rather than dependence," and that "many people, including professionals, do not know how to deal with the handicapped." Indeed, Behm noted that "Blind people are often put into a mold." Behm became a valued employee, as well as an important role model to his peers.

In 1977, Stout, a deaf UWM student, partnered with Bob Tratolli to run DSS's program for students with hearing impairments. (At the time, Tratolli was also coordinator of UWM's Living and Learning Center, a forerunner of the university's Living Learning Communities, a program that offers students with shared interests and experiences the opportunity to live together.) Stout faced several challenges due to her deafness and, according to the *UWM Post*, initially avoided listing her handicap on applications and records because she did not want to experience the "immediate discrimination that many handicapped persons face each day." Said Stout, "If I can get a job, and I'm qualified, I want it. I don't want one to hire me or not hire me because of my impairment."

*UWM commencement exercises, 2019 (left) and 2021. Accessible design initiatives ensured that students with disabilities could participate in commencement in a fashion equal to that of their peers. Photo by Roger O. Smith.*

According to Stout and Tratolli, the biggest struggle for deaf students at UWM was taking notes in class. Even deaf students able to lip read often found classroom learning difficult when professors had facial hair, moved around the room, or faced the blackboard when teaching. Stout worked in the program up to twenty hours a week, scheduling interpreters and enlisting student volunteers to transcribe lecture recordings for use by the sixty students who officially reported hearing impairments to the university. With more resources available, the population of students with disabilities increased. In May 1978, Stout told the *UWM Post* that 293 students with declared disabilities were attending UWM.

In 1984, Martin Armato became the full-time coordinator of DSS's Hearing-Impaired program—the only such program in the state of Wisconsin. Having grown up with a brother who was deaf, Armato had witnessed firsthand the intricacies of the disability and the challenges deaf students might face, and thus provided students on campus with more than just necessary accommodations. For example, in 1985, to help break down communication barriers and eliminate hesitancy on the part of others to connect with deaf students, Armato introduced UWM to what was then Deaf Awareness Week, a national event featuring workshops, exhibits, and performances that, according to the *UWM Post*, were "all designed to heighten awareness

about the deaf community and its culture." Deaf Awareness Week continued to be observed at UWM through 2015.

In 1994, DSS became the Student Accessibility Center (SAC), and UWM continued the trend that saw staff with disabilities leading disability programs. Take for example Don Natzke, who had been directing DSS and assumed the same role at SAC. Natzke, who brought his experience as a person who is blind to an administrative leadership position, later went on to become the executive director of Milwaukee County's Office of Persons with Disabilities.

A landmark national initiative launched in the 1990s with the passage of the Americans with Disabilities Act (ADA). Signed into law in July 1990, the ADA prompted a sweeping cultural change as more architectural and landscape features—such as automatic doorways, ramps, and curb cuts—made disability access more visible. Along with all other public entities, the University of Wisconsin System was required to create an ADA transition plan and regular self-evaluations that formalized system-wide deliberations and documentation related to disability issues. In 1997–1998, Assistant Vice-Chancellor Sona Andrews offered presentations to division directors on accessibility audits designed and completed by students that highlighted the accessibility needs on campus and recommended possible solutions.

Jeb Willenbring (back row left) and Aura Hirschman (back row right) with blind and visually impaired students, 2017.

Also active at the time were two committees: UWM's Americans with Disabilities Advisory Committee, which reported to the chancellor, and the UW System's President's Advisory Committee on Disability Issues (PACDI), which reported directly to the System's president. UWM's representatives on PACDI have included Student Accessibility Center Director Vicky Groser; Professor of Occupational Science & Technology Roger O. Smith; and Christopher Baumann, a graduate student in psychology. (Professor of Physical Therapy, Rehabilitation Sciences & Technology Victoria A. Moerchen joined the committee in 2021.)

Other academic support programs specifically designed for students with learning disabilities or psychological disabilities proliferated between 1997 and 2007, a development that led to a surge in the number of students with disabilities on campus. Today, that figure stands at more than fourteen hundred. Growth in both the range of services provided and the diversity of students with disabilities served led to several positive developments at UWM such as fresh perspectives, new partnerships, improved technology on campus, and greater access to learning.

Another shift occurred in the early 2000s, in part due to the ADA's emphasis on universal accessibility. The terms "universal design,"

"accessibility," and "inclusive design" began to proliferate in education nationally. One of the main components of Chancellor Nancy Zimpher's 1999 series of initiatives known as the Milwaukee Idea was Campus Design Solutions (CDS), later renamed Community Design Solutions. A key project of CDS was the design and construction of the Milwaukee Idea Home (MIH), a state-of-the-art, green, and disability-accessible demonstration home completed in 2004. According to the website of UWM's Rehabilitation Research Design & Disability Center ($R_2D_2$), which conducts research related to technology and disability, and which collaborated on the development of the home, "the MIH was designed for an urban setting, Milwaukee, which has small and narrow lots much like other older cities" and included "affordability, conservation, and accessibility." Chancellor Zimpher personally promoted the accessibility component of the home and the project led to a long-lasting community partnership with Independence First, a local resource center for people with disabilities that for a number of years operated the home as a transitional facility for individuals seeking permanent housing.

As a result of this shift toward universal design, $R_2D_2$ partnered with the UW System's PACDI, receiving almost $2.5 million in awards from the US Department of Education. With this funding, the center launched projects intended to bring accessible design to campus and, in the process, created the world-class web resource ACCESS-ed. As part of the process, students created more than sixty audits of campus programs and facilities and initiated numerous accessibility interventions. For example, students shared accessible designs for the commencement ceremonies with UWM officials, ensuring that all graduates using wheelchairs and other mobility devices could participate in a fashion equal to that of their peers. This work led to the development of fifteen Accessibility and Universal Design Information Tools that remain relevant as accessibility evaluations and marked $R_2D_2$ as a significant contributor to accessibility locally, nationally, and globally.

While the ADA and its accessibility requirements impacted UWM greatly, faculty members in the university's Department of Rehabilitation Sciences & Technology, in turn, have influenced disability-related fields both nationally and internationally. They include Smith, who served as president of the Rehabilitation Engineering and Assistive Technology Society of North America from 2016 to 2018; Associate Professor Virginia Stoffel, who served as president of the American Occupational Therapy Association from 2013 to 2016; and Phyllis King, professor of occupational therapy and associate vice-chancellor in the Division of Academic Affairs, who served as president of the 130-member Association of Schools Advancing Health Professions (ASAHP) from 2019 to 2021.

ASAHP includes 116 universities and 4 professional organizations that host disability-related professional training programs.

As teaching pedagogy adapted to twenty-first century learning, media and online courses became important components in university curricula, and the need for improved electronic accessibility grew. In fiscal year 2008, under the guidance of Ginny Chiaverina, manager of what was then the Deaf and Hard of Hearing Program within SAC, the center secured a $44,855 UWM Educational Technology Grant that was used to acquire both the equipment needed to provide hard of hearing students with transcripts of course lectures and CaptionMaker, a program that made it possible to add captions to media used in the classroom. This postproduction captioning quickly took off, and in 2013, the center hired Fran Lorenz as full-time coordinator of this service. When YouTube became a popular site from which to draw supplemental curricula, demands for captioning rose again, and Lorenz began using volunteers to keep up with demand. Even with the availability of captioning and more efficient access for students, some instructors did not understand the need for captioned media, nor were they aware of how much this and other adjustments in the classroom, in person or online, would greatly improve accessibility for the entire student population.

SAC was renamed the Accessibility Resource Center (ARC) in 2013 and in 2016 began partnering with UWM's Center for Excellence in Teaching and Learning (CETL) to help resolve such resistance from instructors. Together with CETL, ARC created a training package, Accessibility Training for Instructors, for all UWM faculty and staff. This training provided resources for supporting students with disabilities and information about the way principles of universal design could be used to improve access for all students, not just those with disabilities. According to ARC Adaptive Technology Specialist Shannon Aylesworth, "When other institutions in Wisconsin learned of our collaboration and the success of our training, several requested access to the training for their instructional staff." In 2018, the training package

and related resources were made available in Canvas Commons, an online learning repository that enables all educators to find, import, and share resources.

ARC also collaborated with other departments and centers on campus to expand access academically and culturally. For example, in 2016, Aura Hirschman, a counselor in the center, partnered with Professor of Mathematics Jeb Willenbring to design specialized tutoring and technology support for visually impaired students. In a significant initiative funded by what at the time was Industries for the Blind Inc., Hirschman and Willenbring developed an approach that provided students with accessibility tutors using assistive technology. This pilot program helped five students who were blind or visually impaired successfully complete required math courses, with most, according to ARC, receiving As in their respective courses. This project also provided field experience for UWM students in occupational therapy and education; hired as accessibility tutors,

they gained knowledge and skills that translated into their professional careers.

In 2017, the Committee on Accreditation for Rehabilitation Engineering and Assistive Technology Education (CoA-RATE) favorably reviewed UWM's interdepartmental Assistive Technology and Accessible Design Graduate Certificate, leading to the program becoming one of only three accredited training programs in the world. Later, Smith and Aylesworth would both sit on the CoA-RATE Board of Directors. And in 2018, ARC Staff Interpreter Lauren Rado collaborated with Ralph Janes from UWM's Department of Theatre to pilot a program geared toward making the university's theater performances accessible for deaf audiences by bringing American Sign Language to the stage. Rado also mentored a student in ARC's Interpreter Training Program who interpreted a performance of *Book of Days* in April of that year.

Industries for the Blind continued its support for students with disabilities at UWM in 2018 with an $11,000 grant to ARC for the purchase of two closed-circuit television sets, software licenses for university laptops, and two hours of training for ARC staff on the software. The licenses ensured that students had uninterrupted access to university information and course curriculum whether they were on or off campus. Two years later, ARC received a $24,000 grant from what was by then Industries for the Blind and Hearing Impaired Inc. that was earmarked for the purchase of additional equipment such as portable video magnifiers for all three UWM campuses. Moreover, this grant propelled UWM into the leader's circle again by making it the first university in the state to purchase a subscription to the Aira Campus Network, a visual interpreting service. Through an app created by Aira that can be downloaded to a smartphone, anyone on campus who is blind or visually impaired can connect with professional, live agents who help make course materials, navigation services, and food service accessible.

Despite these advances, students with disabilities still faced multiple challenges in finding peer-to-peer connections and social experiences equitable to those of other students. Having created a strong foundation for academic accessibility, ARC established student organizations and programs that opened doors for socializing, networking, and mentoring. In 2014, for example, ARC Interim Director Barbara Simon established the Autism Social Group for students with autism spectrum disorders, who tend to isolate or feel unsure about how to start or carry on conversations with others. The group's meetings allowed students opportunities to discuss classes, work, and weekend plans, as well as engage in group activities.

▲

*Ethiel Vega-Padilla, shown here in a 2021 photo, became a strong advocate for people with disabilities as a result of his experiences at UWM.* Photo courtesy Ethiel Vega-Padilla.

In 2017, Jonathan Broskowski—at the time an ARC counselor (and today, ARC's interim director)—along with Meredith Williams and Andrew Ruzkowski established the ARC Student Group (ASG) to provide students with any disability opportunities to meet and discuss mutual challenges and share successes. According to Broskowski, "Some studies show students with disabilities participate in fewer extracurricular activities, like clubs or on-campus events." He said that could be because "many colleges and university programs focus mainly on academic and physical accessibility."

One year after ASG's formation, Broskowski, Williams, and Ruzkowski laid the groundwork for a partnership with the national organization Disability Rights, Education, Activism, and Mentoring (DREAM), which gave the group access to additional resources such as members-only trainings, Mentor Monday Webinars, and more. The DREAM at UWM chapter also began holding a monthly social hour for students with disabilities.

ARC also established the first cluster of students who were deaf or hard of hearing in the Ignite Leadership Institute, a campus-wide program for students interested in developing leadership skills and creating long-lasting connections. Coaches Jason Anderson, Cassie Franklin, and Amy Hogle, all ARC staff members, and deaf student Teresa Baumgartner, adapted the Ignite curriculum to make a stronger impact for deaf and hard of hearing students so they might, according to ARC, "develop insight into how to become more effective leaders, dispel misconceptions regarding deafness and hearing loss, and learn from each other on how to be better self-advocates."

Research and reports on the history of programs and opportunities for students with disabilities give some insight into the success students achieve at UWM, but the true test of value and impact is found in personal testimonies. Although Tiffany N. Payne began her undergraduate studies at UWM in 1992, she was not new to campus. Payne first became acquainted with UWM when she participated in Upward Bound, the university's four-year-long college prep program. Through Upward Bound, Payne learned of the services offered by DSS. "My choice to connect [with DSS] and utilize the services was based on the fact that one does not achieve success on their own," she said. "An external support system is necessary, and luckily, that's what DSS became for me." After graduation, Payne continued to lean on the "support, lessons, and sentiments" gathered from DSS, saying that her experience at the university was within a "culture of inclusiveness, innovation, collaboration, attention to detail, and an emphasis on people and outcome." She said the department not only fostered her success, self-esteem, self-advocacy skills, and networking skills, but also "partnerships and friendships that have lasted decades."

Ethiel Vega-Padilla chose UWM because it was close to home and affordable. Faced with the difficulty of adjusting to classes and workloads, Vega-Padilla applied for accommodations. "The impact that accommodations had [was] positive as it leveled the playing field," he said. "Having someone take notes while I could pay attention to what the professor had to say was pivotal to my success." He also noted that advocacy plays a huge role in succeeding. "Advocacy . . . brought me closer to connecting to the disability culture at UWM and experiencing it firsthand with the startup of the student organization DREAM. I quickly became an integral member and from

▲

*Meredith Williams, shown here in a 2021 photo, found UWM to be the only one of several colleges she attended that provided the support and accommodations she needed to succeed.* Photo courtesy Meredith Williams.

then on, my advocacy for people with disabilities evolved into one of the most important characteristics of my being." Vega-Padilla defines the disability culture as one that has "grit and moxie," and his participation in DREAM proved his own "power of perseverance and strong will to achieve anything."

Another DREAM leader at UWM is Meredith Williams, who lives with a rare autoinflammatory condition that makes college attendance and participation challenging. "It took nine years and four different colleges to receive my undergraduate degree," she said, "mostly due to lack of understanding of the experience of students with chronic illnesses and disabilities, and a lack of available accommodations." Williams said UWM was the first college she attended that not only provided the level of support and necessary accommodations she needed, but also reduced the amount of resistance she encountered from instructors. "At UWM, I was finally able to complete my undergraduate education and graduate with honors," said. "After receiving my [master's degree in public health] elsewhere, I was eager to return to UWM for my PhD program based on the positive experiences I had as a student with disabilities during undergrad." Williams's involvement with DREAM has been one of her most rewarding experiences at UWM. "Other people with disabilities can be difficult to find at universities for a number of reasons—it is much harder for people with disabilities to go to college and to stay in college once they are admitted, and a lot of us, particularly in PhD programs, are afraid to be 'out' and disclose our disabilities." DREAM gave Williams a chance to be herself and to connect with others who had similar experiences and frustrations. "We really try to validate the concerns and experiences of other students, embrace and celebrate disability as a positive, vibrant aspect of diversity on campus, and amplify the scientific, cultural, and social contributions that students with disabilities make on campus."

Jason Anderson, a UWM alum and ARC access specialist, never planned on attending college. After a case of spinal meningitis at a very young age left him deaf in his left ear and with significant hearing loss in the right, Anderson struggled in school. Eventually, he dropped out and began struggling in the workforce. When he lost the remaining hearing in his right ear and became totally deaf, Anderson wondered how he would communicate with others. Holding a job seemed impossible. Anderson sought help from the Wisconsin Division of Vocational Rehabilitation (DVR), earned his high school equivalency diploma, and in 2007 at age twenty-five was accepted as a student at UWM. Recalled Anderson, "DVR was incredibly helpful by pointing me in the right direction, and I found the staff at UWM to be warm and welcoming . . . but the one thing that loomed over my head was just how I was going to be able to understand the lectures." Uncertain that SAC could provide him worthwhile assistance, Anderson was surprised to find that Franklin, his student advisor in what was then the Deaf and Hard of Hearing Program, was deaf herself. Yet he still was not convinced she could offer him a solution.

"Cassie told me to hold on and left the room for a moment," recalled Anderson. "She returned with a laptop and another person while I sat there, confused about what was happening. The other person placed the laptop in front of me and then sat down at her own computer. Cassie began to speak and gestured for me to look at the screen. Words began to appear on the screen, and it took me a moment to realize what was happening." Continued Anderson, "Cassie was speaking and explaining that the university offers captioning services to students that do not sign and need to have access to communication. Someone must have been cutting a lot of onions in that room,

*UWM alum Jason Anderson, shown here in a 2021 photo, works as an ARC access specialist.*

because all [of a] sudden my eyes started leaking. It was the strangest thing."

Franklin became the most important person in Anderson's life during that time, teaching him about deafness and the ADA, and about the importance of advocating for himself. Anderson joined UWM's Americans with Disabilities Advisory Committee as a student representative. He enrolled in several American Sign Language classes, built strong connections with other deaf people on campus, and earned an internship at Independence First. Later, after graduating from UWM, he was hired to take Cassie Franklin's place when she took on another position on campus. "My first day, I sat on the other side of the very desk where I had begun my journey," Anderson recalled. "It was now my turn to act as a guide for others navigating the world of higher education and deafness."

There are many more stories of faculty, staff, and students who continue to create the reasons students from all cultures and abilities attend UWM—success stories that can be traced not only to decades of disability programming on campus but also to the forward thinking, leadership, discovery, and commitment promulgated by a disability-inclusive culture. As the student population becomes even more diverse—and UWM's culture even more inclusive—the university's disability-related instructional, research, and service programs are poised to respond. While universities nationwide struggle to meet the challenge of providing equitable higher education for students with disabilities, such students in the Milwaukee community may rest assured that they will find at UWM the support, encouragement, and advocacy they need to acquire a premier college experience.

CHAPTER

8

# International Diversity at UWM: History and Perspectives

TRACY BUSS AND
DEVARAJAN VENUGOPALAN

*University of Wisconsin-Milwaukee (UWM) students participating in a study abroad program in Belize led by Anika Wilson (back, left), associate professor, African and African Diaspora Studies, summer 2017.*

Since its founding, the University of Wisconsin-Milwaukee (UWM), a research university intent on providing access to its urban population, has worked toward internationalization. In 1961, the University of Wisconsin Board of Regents affirmed the following:

> We recognize that the university's first responsibility is to Wisconsin and its residents. But the university must look outward if this obligation is to be fulfilled. Thus, we as Regents, declare that the university should welcome students from foreign lands. These out-of-state students are an educational and cultural asset to our Wisconsin students and make a substantial economic contribution to our state.

> The University's contribution to international understanding also shall include exchange of students and faculty official visits, research applicable to problems of underdeveloped countries, and similar functions it is uniquely able to perform. The interdependence of the world's people, the ease of travel and communication, the rising importance of other cultures, and the quest for peace have tended to make the globe our campus. This trend we encourage.

J. Martin Klotsche, UWM's visionary first chancellor, was an internationally minded scholar who broadened his own global perspective by accepting an assignment in 1967–1968 to lead a study of higher education in Brazil. In Klotsche's 1966 annual address, he had formally announced that he would be away for extended periods of time over the following year and a half. He also expressed his plan to create a campus internationalization strategy that would be thoughtful and long range, not "willy-nilly." Other universities had made the mistake, said Klotsche, of "separating their international programs from the mainstream of university life" and this "isolated them from the rest of the university."

As a result, UWM's campus internationalization has been rooted in the philosophy that students, faculty, and staff all benefit from international activities that span a wide range, including but not limited to, international student recruitment, short- and long-term study abroad, academic program and course development, international interinstitutional partnerships, and outreach in the community. This comprehensive approach to internationalization has been a key contributor to making UWM a diverse, welcoming, and inclusive campus.

In the words of the urban studies theorist Richard Florida, "Higher-education institutions are also the community entities that, perhaps more than any other, have opened up city after city and college town after college town to the world. In this respect, they are bastions and breeders of tolerance. A university, with its tendency toward openness to ideas, people, and practices not always considered mainstream, is a natural source of diversity—whether ethnic, socio-economic, or cultural. . . ." To that end, UWM has continually strived to attract and retain qualified international students through international institutional partnerships, recruitment initiatives, faculty relationships, and reputation. By 1984, the number of international students was already quite impressive—1,096 international students from a wide array of countries were enrolled at UWM. This number has ebbed and flowed over the years, with the highest level of enrollment at 1,612 international students in fall 2015. As of fall 2020, in the midst of a global pandemic that challenged international travel and made student visas extremely difficult to obtain, 1,017 international students from more than 80 countries enrolled.

Jill Cherny, an advisor during the 1980s in UWM's Foreign Student Services Office and later its Department of International Studies and Programs, shared her thoughts on the contributions of international student diversity to the campus and Milwaukee community. Said Cherny, "I've been told that a university cannot be a true university unless there is representation from other cultures. I also know that people think of this campus as simply a commuter school, but the growing numbers of foreign and out-of-state students are a strong message that UWM brings the world to Milwaukee, and we are much richer for it."

In the early 1970s, UWM faculty members in linguistics worked to establish UWM's English as a Second Language (ESL) program. (An ESL program was also being offered at that time through the Spanish Speaking Outreach Institute.) Senior Lecturer Peter Lee, who worked from 1977 to 2005 in what was by then the Intensive English as a Second Language Program, recounted that by the middle to late 1980s, the program saw a large influx of students, many Chinese, but also students from approximately thirty-five other countries. Students participated in activities such as a cultural partners program in collaboration with what was then UWM's Communication Department

connecting ESL students with native-speaking undergraduates. Similar activities continue today, with students receiving English language instruction through UWM's English Language Academy. The academy offers both an Intensive English Program (IEP) for students who need to improve their English skills prior to commencing degree-seeking study, and English for Academic Purposes courses for students admitted into degree programs.

Some students, such as Father Jorge Hernández, for example, study in the IEP program in preparation for non-UWM degree programs. Hernández's reason for coming to UWM from Colombia in 2005 to build his English skills was particularly unique; he enrolled in its ESL program in preparation for earning a master's degree in divinity and becoming a Catholic priest for the Archdiocese of Milwaukee. "UWM was very welcoming, and it was the right place for me because it helped me find friends from here and all over the world," recalled Hernández. "As I learned to communicate in English over time, the more welcoming and greater experience I received. I truly enjoyed my time at UWM."

During the 1980s, when on-campus housing was in short supply, some generous Milwaukee residents opened their arms to host international students for home stays. A 1985 UWM press release described the home of one such resident, Marie Brundage, as "a familiar abode for international students" from countries such as Korea, Japan, India, Bangladesh, Italy, Venezuela, and Yemen. A young couple from the South Side profiled in the *Milwaukee Journal*, Gayle and Michael La Pinske, provided not only a home but also tuition to Chang Yung-ti, a student Gayle La Pinske had met while on a UWM study trip in China. These experiences allowed the host families to gain intimate knowledge of many cultures, traveling no further than their front door.

Home stays for international students are not as common

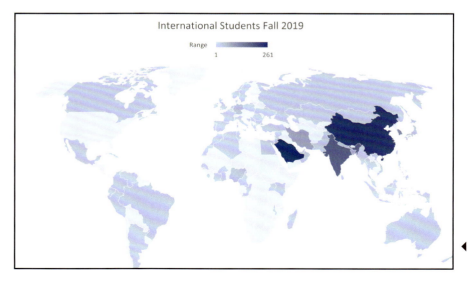

International Students Fall 2019

Range
1          261

◄ Map showing countries of origin of international students attending UWM, 2019.

*Chancellor Carlos E. Santiago speaking to international students at the UWM Center for International Education's Fall Welcome Reception, 2006. Photo courtesy Brooke Thomas.*

now as they were in UWM's earlier years, and international students living in on- and off-campus housing find connections and receive support from a variety of sources, including campus student services offices, academic departments, advising staff, faculty, and student organizations. International Student and Scholar Services (ISSS) at UWM's Center for International Education (CIE) is often the first office to be in contact with international students through recruitment efforts such as fairs and information sessions. ISSS provides assistance to students as they submit their applications to UWM and later navigate their journey to Milwaukee after their admission. Once they arrive on campus, international students find ISSS to be a continuous source of support that offers advising on immigration and adjustment issues and provides a social network by sponsoring social events and "buddy" programs. The goal is

to find ways to bridge the gap that sometimes exists between international students and students from Wisconsin or other parts of the United States. Some events designed to bring students together have included Thanksgiving dinners, movies, outings such as ski trips and Black Friday shopping excursions, culturally themed coffee and tea hours, and a popular Harry Potter-themed Halloween party complete with costumed staff members and a fortune teller—an annual event held in Greene Hall.

Kemal Pelit, who earned a bachelor's degree in civil engineering in 2006, shared his memories of being a new international student from Turkey:

> I remember being a young man who wasn't very sure of himself. I was eighteen at the time and I had left my country, my hometown, for the very first time. [I'd] left my friends behind. . . . Although I could understand English, I wasn't as fluid as I have become over the years. Communicating was difficult and making friends was even harder at times. It took me some time to gain my footing both academically and socially in an environment that was completely different from what I have grown accustomed to. Despite the challenges that I have faced, the cultural

*International students at an ice cream social sponsored by UWM's International Student and Scholar Services in Greene Hall, fall 2017. Photo courtesy Sue Conway.*

fabric of the UWM, and perhaps the Midwest, had made it possible for me to make new friends, [and] achieve academic success, and [I] left Milwaukee as an adult who was ready to face new challenges.

Faculty and staff have played an essential role in attracting talented international students to UWM, making them feel welcome on campus, helping them succeed, and serving as both mentors and friends they could talk to. Consider, for example, that many of UWM's research scientists (59 of whom were among the top 2 percent of scientists in the world, according to a study by Stanford University) have balanced their research activity with supervising significant numbers of graduate students. Wilmeth Professor and Distinguished Professor of Economics Mohsen Bahmani-Oskooee perhaps sets the record, chairing fifty-three PhD committees for students from countries such as Iran, Mexico, Korea, the Philippines, India, Tunisia, Taiwan, Pakistan, Ethiopia, Thailand, Bangladesh, Albania, Turkey, Greece, Malaysia, Russia, Egypt, and Kenya.

Professor Emeritus of Economics Swarnjit Arora, whose career at UWM began in 1972, recalled that during his early years on campus there were a significant number of students from Germany and Mexico, and that later UWM would welcome more students from India and China. Indeed, as UWM's faculty became more diverse, so did its

*Associate Professor of Biomedical and Mechanical Engineering Mohammad Rahman with students in his BioRobotics Lab, 2018.*

international student body. Shepard House, which had been quarters for Peace Corps volunteers, was a gathering place for international students. Faculty, including Arora, volunteered their time to help international students get settled in, even picking them up from the airport. Although airport pickup eventually came to be organized by ISSS, UWM faculty remain very engaged in providing support to students.

Neel Kamal Chapagain, from Nepal, came to UWM to pursue a PhD in architecture, which he earned in 2011. With a strong interest in cultural heritage, Chapagain found Milwaukee to be a "good urban lab" where he could "enhance my understanding of cultural diversity of the United States." He cites, as particularly valuable, opportunities afforded by Community Design Solutions—a center at the School of Architecture & Urban Planning—to "practice my core interest areas like community participation, participatory design, and everyday cultural heritage." Elaborating on the multiple constructs of diversity that he experienced on campus and in the Milwaukee community, he notes that his cohort group included students who were Southeast and East Asian and American Indian, as well as Midwestern; there were also faculty members

*Students having fun with calligraphy at the International Student Bazaar sponsored by the Global Student Alliance, fall 2010.*

with backgrounds in architecture, anthropology, psychology, and urban studies. Today, Chapagain directs the Centre for Heritage Management at India's Ahmedabad University and works with organizations such as UNESCO and multiple academic networks. "Some of the values and experiences I gained during my studies in the United States have been always helpful," he says. "I am grateful for such a wonderful experience."

Faculty and staff have also offered their time as advisors to UWM student organizations. As of 2020, UWM could boast of sponsoring approximately three hundred such groups, all founded and led by students and funded in part by the university. These organizations have represented a wide variety of interests across campus, increasing awareness of other cultures and supporting international and domestic students alike. The African Student Association, Asian Student Union, the now-defunct Bangladesh Student Association, Chinese Student and Scholar Association, Global Student Alliance, Taiwanese Student Association, and the Student Association of India are just a few of the student organizations that have taken an active role in supporting international students and increasing awareness of their culture. Designed to do just that is Korea Day, a particularly popular event organized by the Korean American Faculty and Staff Association at UWM and the Korean American Association of Milwaukee.

Each international student in the UWM community can speak to having his or her own unique experience and has contributed to UWM's diversity in a wide variety of ways—by engaging in the classroom, participating in storytelling, volunteering across campus, and merely being present. Magdalena Irigaray from Argentina, who earned a bachelor's degree in international studies and a Latin American and Caribbean Studies Certificate in 2003, noted that "it's hard to measure one's contribution at a large scale but I guess I was making an impact just by being there, by making my country's uniqueness visible, and by participating in activities and events where my voice was heard. Representation matters at any level."

UWM students have been studying abroad since the 1960s and the university's study abroad and exchange programs have provided pivotal opportunities for students to explore diversity and identity. CIE, founded in 2000, supports such programs in more than forty countries on six continents and maintains bilateral exchanges with more than twenty universities. Short-term, faculty-led programs have been a popular model for students, especially for many who may find it difficult to be away for a semester or year due to financial or family concerns.

*Professor of Economics Swarnjit Arora (front row, far left) with study abroad students at the Golden Temple in Amritsar, India, 1999.* Photo courtesy Swarnjit Arora.

First-generation, racial minority students, and students with disabilities have traditionally been underrepresented in study abroad programs; UWM has endeavored to encourage them to take part, providing individualized advising by staff and peers and financial support in the form of grants and scholarships. In 2012, UWM established the Diversity in Study Abroad Scholarship, administered collaboratively by what was then the Division of Global Inclusion & Engagement, CIE, and the Office of the Provost.

UWM faculty members' longstanding support of short-term study abroad programs that take place over summer, UWinteriM, and spring break have given thousands of students the chance to learn about other countries and cultures and develop valuable skills through experiential learning. Almost all UWM's schools and colleges have faculty-led programs, such as the long-running program to Ghana through the Department of African and African Diaspora Studies (formerly Africology) in the College of Letters & Science. Offered since 2002, this program has introduced students to the culture, politics, and economics of Ghana and the region of West Africa. For many Black students in particular, this program has represented a chance to return "home" and explore their African heritage.

Myriad additional programs have served students over the years and demonstrate the breadth of faculty-led programs offered by UWM. The College of Letters & Science has supported numerous language learning and cultural immersion programs in France, Ireland, Italy, Japan, Morocco, and Spain. UWM's oldest summer school program, led by Professor of Foreign Languages and Literature Michael Mikos, gives students a chance to practice their Polish language skills and experience life in Poland. Professor of Mathematical Sciences Jonathan Kahl has taken students to Mexico since 2010 to study the effect of air pollution on ancient cultural ruins. The United Nations Summer Seminar, led by Professor of Political Science Shale Horowitz and focusing on international relations, international organizations, and the United Nations, has been offered since 1966. The College of Nursing has supported community health care and wellness programs in Malawi, led by Professor Lucy Mkandawire-Valhmu; in Kenya, led by Associate Professor Peninnah Kako; and in Ecuador, led by Assistant Professor Heidi Luft and Associate Professor Teresa Johnson. Additionally, Professor of Nursing Julia Snethen has led a program focusing on the health of women and children in Thailand since 2014.

*Professor of History Chia Youyee Vang (front row, second from right) with study abroad students at the Plain of Jars, Laos, 2011. Photo courtesy Chia Youyee Vang.*

Other faculty running study abroad programs include Simone Ferro, professor of dance in the Peck School of the Arts, who has led multiple trips to Brazil exploring African influences in Brazilian culture. Faculty from the Helen Bader School of Social Welfare have led comparative social work policy programs and programs on other topics in Austria, South Africa, and Costa Rica. The School of Architecture and Urban Planning has sponsored annual programs to Europe, Japan, and Cuba. The Sheldon B. Lubar School of Business sponsors faculty-led programs in various countries throughout Europe and Asia exploring global business practices. The College of Engineering & Applied Science has offered long-standing programs in Germany and Taiwan. The School of Education has supported sign language and deaf culture immersion programs in France, Italy, and the United Kingdom. Each of these programs has offered unique opportunities for students to learn in diverse environments and UWM's faculty members have been the driving force behind their success.

Navee Lor (BS, molecular biology; Hmong Diaspora Studies Certificate, 2018) participated in a short-term study abroad program to Cambodia, Laos, and Vietnam in 2018 led by then-Associate Vice-Chancellor in the Division of Global Inclusion & Engagement and Professor of History Chia Youyee Vang. Lor shared her thoughts after her return:

> Visiting the country that my family came from for the first time was surreal. If there are three things that I have taken away from this trip [they are] (1) the meaning of sacrifice, (2) my Hmong privileges, and (3) a deeper appreciation for my Hmong American identity. I have always associated sacrifice with my sleep,

*Assistant Professor of Nursing Anne Dressel (far right) with study abroad students learning about traditional healing methods in Tena, Ecuador, summer 2019. Photo courtesy Anne Dressel.*

comfort, and time. Though these are real sacrifices for me, they become small and almost irrational when compared to what my parents and the women in Sapa sacrifice on a daily basis. . . . These experiences have challenged me to redefine and reevaluate how I perceive privilege and more importantly, confront my own.

Study abroad has been a transformative experience for students like Lor. As just one more example, Violeta Ramirez, who earned a bachelor's degree in global studies and a Peace Studies Certificate in 2020, and who worked in CIE as a student, was inspired by her experiences studying abroad in Japan and South Korea and went on to a first post-graduation job working in the Center for International Education at the College of Lake County, her alma mater prior to UWM.

Undergraduate students have also engaged in research abroad that was supported by grants from UWM's Office of Undergraduate Research. For example, in July 2011, Kako and Patricia

Stevens, professors of nursing, collected data in rural eastern Kenya as part of an ongoing study, "HIV Transmission Risk, Treatment, and Illness Management Over Time: An In-Depth Longitudinal Study of HIV-Infected Women in Kenya," funded by the UWM Graduate School and other sources. Kako and Stevens were assisted by students Victoria Scheer—who earned a bachelor's degree and PhD in nursing in 2011 and 2022, respectively—and Sarah Slivon, who earned her bachelor's degree in nursing in 2012 and PhD in nursing in 2020.

As an urban research university providing access to high-quality international education for a nontraditional student body, UWM has paved the way for the state and the nation. UWM's major in international studies, for example, was the first interdisciplinary international studies program in Wisconsin. Since 1957, it has prepared graduates for advanced studies and careers in international relations and economic development. Professor of Political Science Donald Shea was appointed as UWM's first Dean of International Studies and Programs in December 1956.

Professor of Political Science and former Faculty Coordinator of International Studies Donald Pienkos recalled that in late 1970 a group of UWM faculty met to discuss their shared interest in teaching and research in Russian and East European studies, which led to the creation

*Associate Professor of Nursing Peninnah Kako (far right) and students Sarah Slivon and Victoria Scheer outside a rural church in Kenya. They are accompanied by the area chief (left of Kako) after a community leaders' focus group meeting on the impact of HIV/AIDS in the local community, 2011.* Photo courtesy Peninnah Kako.

organizes conferences and programs; offers courses, certificates, and degrees in global health; and fosters global health research.

Foreign language offerings—including French, German, Italian, Spanish, and less-commonly taught languages such as Arabic, Chinese, Hebrew, Hmong, Irish Gaelic, Japanese, Korean, Polish, Portuguese, and Russian—have long been one of UWM's academic assets. Its Language Resource Center, a unit of the College of Letters & Science, provides valuable instructional resources (many created by student interns) for students as well as professional development opportunities for language instructors.

UWM's Golda Meir Library, home to the American Geographical Society Library (AGSL) since it was relocated from New York in 1978, contains an extensive collection of well over 1.5 million items including maps, atlases, books, journals, pamphlets, photographs, slides, Landsat satellite images, and digital spatial data. It is one of the premier collections of its kind in North America. Visiting delegations from abroad often visit the AGSL, where they are invited to view displays of maps of their home countries not available elsewhere. Scholars from around the world have participated in the AGS Library fellowship program.

UWM's array of international academic programs and resources has been considerably strengthened by prestigious funding awarded CIE by the US Department of Education under Title VI of the Higher Education Act—funding that since CIE's inception has totaled close to $5 million. Additionally, CLACS, a Title VI National Resource since 1965, has received more than $4.8 million in federal funds. This funding has supported student foreign language study and study abroad, course development, and outreach activities with the stated goal of broadening access to students traditionally underrepresented in international

of an array of internationally focused certificate programs in disciplines such as Asian Studies, French and Francophone Studies, Latin American and Caribbean Studies, Middle Eastern and North African Studies, and Peace and Conflict Studies. These certificate programs, similar to a minor, have allowed students over the years to add an international aspect to their UWM studies.

UWM launched an innovative Global Studies bachelor's degree program in 2003—the first of its kind in the nation—administered by CIE up until 2018–2019 and initially supported by funding from Chancellor Nancy Zimpher's Milwaukee Idea initiative at the behest of Governor Tommy Thompson. The Global Studies program incorporated some ambitious curricular requirements: study abroad for the equivalent of one semester, multiple semesters of foreign language, and an overseas internship. Some wondered if UWM's students, many of whom are first-generation students from underrepresented and socioeconomically diverse groups, would choose Global Studies. In fact, by fall 2010, during a period of peak enrollment, more than two hundred students were enrolled in Global Studies, some of whom had never before traveled outside of the Midwest.

The Center for Latin American and Caribbean Studies (CLACS) at UWM is home to a major in Latin American, Caribbean, and US Latinx Studies that integrates the study of the region with that of Latinx people within the United States. UWM's Center for Global Health Equity in the College of Nursing coordinates global health study abroad programs; hosts visiting international scholars;

education. In 2021, CIE was awarded an Increase and Diversify Education Abroad for US Students grant from the US State Department's Capacity Building Program for US Study Abroad to support an online course, Black Lives Matter: A Global Comparative Study, and a study abroad program looking at the Black experience in the United States and internationally.

Through the cultivation of international institutional partnerships, UWM has taken an intentional approach to building relationships with universities worldwide, welcoming their students to UWM and providing them with more options for studying abroad. As of 2020, UWM had nearly two hundred such partnership agreements with institutions in forty-eight countries in place. Some of UWM's most active partnerships have been with institutions such as Chung Yuan Christian University and National Taiwan Normal University, in Taiwan; Hubei University of Technology and North China Electric Power University, in China; Justus Liebig University Giessen, in Germany; Mission

▲

*UWM Provost Johannes Britz, Milwaukee Alderman Joe Davis Sr., and others at a signing ceremony for an agreement with South Africa's University of Zululand, July 2010.*

Interuniversitaire de Coordination des Echanges Franco-Américains, in France; Seijo University, in Japan; and the University of Pretoria in South Africa.

Meanwhile, UWM's Institute of World Affairs (IWA) had been founded in 1960 to provide outreach for the community and its educational institutions; today, after merging with CIE in 2003, it remains the only Wisconsin affiliate of the World Affairs Councils of America, an independent, non-partisan organization dedicated to engaging the public in global issues. And in 1963, the Peace Corps

*Professor of Electrical Engineering David Yu (far left) is shown here with Julia Chiu of Chung Yuan Christian University (CYCU) in Taiwan, CYCU students studying at UWM, and staff from the College of Engineering & Applied Science, 2019.* Photo courtesy Julia Chiu.

▼

*Youth in Action's Iron Board Café members visiting campus to explore how the United Nations's Sustainable Development Goals relate to Milwaukee as part of the Preparing Future Global Educators program, 2019.*

requested that UWM create a training program for volunteers, a successful initiative that led to a long-term contract designating UWM as one of only four universities recognized as a year-round Peace Corps Training Center. Although the center closed in 1970, its operation served as the starting point for future international outreach initiatives at UWM, including the formation of CLACS.

Public programs, K–12 outreach initiatives, and teaching and learning resources are all part of efforts by IWA and CLACS to make information on global issues available and accessible to diverse audiences. A core piece of their teacher, youth, and community programs has been the interweaving of the local and global to highlight shared experiences and challenges. For example, IWA's engagement with the Milwaukee Public Schools, overwhelmingly comprised of racial minority students, has included initiatives such as Global Action for Engagement summer programs, global-to-local service learning, and global citizenship curriculum development.

Additionally, IWA has been hosting the Wisconsin High School Model United Nations conference on UWM's campus since 1969. And

the institute's public programs—the Kennan Lectures, Fireside Forum speaker series, and *International Focus* television show—have allowed campus and community members to explore a range of complex global issues from a variety of perspectives. Meanwhile, CLACS initiated its Latin American Film Series in 1979, making it perhaps the longest-running film series in Milwaukee. Some of CLACS's programs to support teachers have included Fulbright-Hays Group Projects Abroad, the Américas Award Book Collection Workshops, and Summer Teacher Institutes.

UWM has played a very important role in the professional growth of many international students, scholars, and others who have come to UWM. For example, Provost and Vice-Chancellor for Academic Affairs Johannes Britz arrived on campus from South Africa as a Visiting Scholar in 2001. Britz vividly remembers not only the helpful assistance he received from the international students' office regarding his visa questions, but also his

sense of feeling connected to the natural beauty of the campus area, the tree-filled neighborhood and parks with Lake Michigan nearby. He has set an example for us by embracing the Wisconsin winters, biking to work through the snow and ice and even regularly swimming in the lake's near-freezing cold water. Britz has shared the kinds of experiences that unite the diverse individuals who have made UWM and Milwaukee their home. While a wide array of internationalization initiatives has contributed to making UWM a more diverse campus, it is UWM's people, and their connections to each other and the campus, who will sustain a welcoming and supportive environment for all.

*International students wearing their country sashes at the Center for International Education graduation party, May 2019.* Photo courtesy Sue Conway.

CHAPTER

9

# The Veteran and Military-Related Experience at UWM: Students, Advisors, and Advocates

Heidi L. Plach,
Yolanda Medina,
Joseph A. Rodríguez, and
Virginia Stoffel

*Military and Veteran Resource Center (MAVRC) staff members at Veterans Day event featuring American flags on Ernest Spaights Plaza, 2019. Photo by Elora Hennessey.*

From its establishment in 1956 and throughout its history, the University of Wisconsin-Milwaukee (UWM) has been a part of the national trend that saw college campuses embrace the presence of military service members and veterans. This presence has not only enriched the campus in terms of diversity of experience, thought, advocacy, and service, but also made UWM a desirable educational destination for each generation of veterans and other military-related students (and their dependents), such as those in active service or the Reserve Officers' Training Corps (ROTC). Though student veterans returning home from service had different experiences (e.g., some had been drafted, others were part of an all-voluntary force), they all echoed a common theme. Richard Herzfeld, a UWM student and US Air Force veteran, said in 1967 that he and his peers had "matured in a way that neither the streets of Brooklyn nor the farms of Wisconsin, nor any other facet of the American way of life could have fostered." Efforts continue to this day to ensure that veterans such as Herzfeld find UWM a place where they fit in, feel they belong, and can enjoy the camaraderie of their peers.

The presence of military and veteran students on campuses all over the United States was facilitated by implementation of the Servicemen's Readjustment Act, commonly known as the GI Bill, which provided educational benefits to service members, veterans, and their families. Signing the bill into law in 1944, President Franklin D. Roosevelt said it was designed to "give servicemen and women the opportunity of resuming their education or technical training after discharge, or of taking a refresher or re-trainer course." (The law also provided additional benefits, such as low-cost mortgages and low-interest business loans to veterans.)

By the time the original GI Bill ended in 1956, almost half of all World War II veterans had participated in the program. (However, Black veterans, due primarily to racism, had a much harder time receiving GI benefits—such as educational grants and loans to start businesses and buy houses—than their white peers.) President George H. W. Bush summed up the impact of the bill in 1990, noting that in the seventy-five years since its passage it had "changed the lives of millions by replacing old roadblocks with paths of opportunity." The GI Bill has seen several extensions and adaptations, including the Veterans' Readjustment Benefits Act of 1966, which provided funds retroactively to more than ten million veterans who had entered the service after the Korean War and to Vietnam War veterans.

*Richard Herzfeld, a US Air Force veteran and University of Wisconsin-Milwaukee (UWM) student, 1967.* Photo courtesy Guy Porth.

Decal - Courtesy of Al Hunsicker

*UWM Vets' Club logo, 1957.* Photo courtesy Guy Porth.

*UWM alum and veteran Lloyd Steiner with the Vets' Club flag, handmade by his mother and displayed down Wisconsin Avenue in many homecoming parades.* Photo by Elora Hennessey.

More recently, the Post-9/11 Veterans Educational Assistance Act of 2008 and the Harry W. Colmery Veterans Educational Assistance Act of 2017—commonly known as the Forever GI Bill—expanded education benefits for even more vets.

A number of factors helped draw veterans to UWM, created from the merger of the University of Wisconsin Extension Division in Milwaukee and Wisconsin State College, Milwaukee in 1956. By then, Milwaukee was home to thousands of veterans of World War II and the Korean War, which had ended just three years earlier. They had been drawn to the city, in part, by a Veterans Administration (VA) Regional Office, a VA hospital, and a cemetery for veterans. For them, UWM proved to be a conveniently located undergraduate option to the University of Wisconsin's main campus ninety miles away in Madison. UWM's lower tuition also attracted veterans, who in 1956–1957 made up 23 percent (1,032 out of 4,481 students) of all undergraduates. Over the next few years, the number of student veterans held steady, at around one thousand, but represented a relatively smaller percentage of overall enrollment as UWM's total student population surged. Those student veterans, who tended to be older than most other undergraduates, founded what would become UWM's longest-running student club, the UWM Vets' Club, a merger of the existing clubs for veterans at UWM's predecessor institutions. In 1957, membership totaled about 150, a figure that dropped to 84 in 1966.

Herzfeld described the UWM Vets' Club as "primarily a social club," noting that "this does not preclude other charitable or self-rewarding activities." Herzfeld recalled club events such as its annual All-School Homecoming celebration featuring a parade down Wisconsin Avenue and a dance, a Christmas Orphans Toy Drive, and intramural sports competitions. He recalled that members "weren't above raising a little hell" and were among the first students through the doors at the grand opening of UWM's Gasthaus, a beer bar, in 1968. Lloyd Steiner, a veteran who that same year received a bachelor's degree in accounting, recalled that student veterans enjoyed socializing and connecting at the Gasthaus. (Given that one had to be twenty-one to drink or serve alcoholic beverages in Milwaukee County at the time, veterans made up most of the Gasthaus's patrons and bartenders.)

In a more serious vein, Vets' Club members engaged in community service. For example, they also were active in student government, with Jim Barnes and Tom Katisch elected president of the UWM Student Association in 1964 and 1965, respectively. Postgraduation, some club members took jobs as instructors at UWM. Rollie Pieper, for example, graduated with a bachelor's degree in business administration in 1970 and taught in that program for six years before enrolling in law school and becoming an attorney. It's significant that despite their vast experiences, multiple veterans cited teaching at UWM among their proudest achievements.

*UWM student and veteran Rollie Pieper studying, circa 1967.*

*UWM student and veteran Guy Porth with the Vets' Club flag, circa 1968. Photo courtesy Guy Porth.*

*Vets' Club Memorabilia. Photo by Elora Hennessey.*

The Vets' Club today continues to help connect more than one hundred former students (and sometimes their spouses) from across the country via email lists, social media, and an annual summer reunion picnic that typically draws about twenty participants. Guy Porth and Douglas "Radar" Lueck have helped maintain the club's archives and, over the years, have organized monthly luncheons for local members. Today, membership is free—compared with the 1962 fee of $1.50 per semester. The sustainability of this group speaks to the value veterans place on staying socially connected through shared life experiences and camaraderie. Ned Redding and Pat Eisenhart, for example, have stayed in touch since graduating from UWM in 1967. Redding went on to become an educator in Milwaukee's central city who mentored countless young students. After a scholarship changed the course of Eisenhart's life, he spent decades working in social services.

The Vietnam War famously divided the nation, and as a result, its veterans did not receive the homecoming parades that had greeted service personnel returning from World War II. Instead, many Vietnam veterans came back to virtually empty airports, greeted only by their closest family members. Moreover, while World War II and

Korean War War veterans returned to a growing national economy, Vietnam veterans faced a tight job market and rising inflation. Drug and alcohol problems persisted among Vietnam veterans, along with what is now recognized as post-traumatic stress disorder (PTSD). Media coverage of these physical and emotional problems led Vietnam veterans to feel alienated, with those on college campuses—the sites of often violent anti-war demonstrations—in many cases feeling estranged from younger undergraduates and some instructors.

Meanwhile, the number of veterans receiving GI benefits had been on the decline, falling to seventy-five by 1965. However, with the passage of the Veterans' Readjustment Benefits Act of 1966, the number of UWM students receiving veterans' benefits soared to more than one thousand during the 1966–1967 academic year. For the first time, the benefits—which initially included direct payments of between $100 and $150 a month (depending on

*UWM Vets' Club members at one of the club's annual picnics representing all six service branches. Left to right: Doug Boerner, US Navy; Archie Arestides, US Army; Pat Eisenhart, US Coast Guard; Guy Porth, US Air Force; Ned Redding, US Marine Corps. Photo courtesy Guy Porth.*

UWM Vets' Club annual picnic, 2021. Photo by Elora Hennessey.

the number of dependents claimed) and increased gradually over time—were extended to military personnel on active duty.

Once on campus, some veterans joined their non-military peers to form organizations determined to end the Vietnam War. In 1967, for example, Veterans for Peace, Students for a Democratic Society, and the Committee on Conscientious Objectors and the Draft united with other student groups to oppose campus visits by recruiters for the US Central Intelligence Agency and what was then the Dow Chemical Company, for a time the military's sole supplier of napalm, a chemical defoliant used to make bombs. The Vietnam Veterans Against the War (VVAW) established a branch at UWM in the early 1970s, educating students about the war, offering advice on financial aid and medical care at the VA, protesting the dishonorable discharge designation, and sponsoring anti-war demonstrations. The largest such protest occurred during the week of April 30, 1970, after President Richard M. Nixon announced that the United States had invaded Cambodia. A weeklong series of protests included a sleep-in on the Mitchell Hall lawn, marches from campus to the Milwaukee Civic Center and War Memorial downtown, showings of the film *Winter Soldier,* classroom lobbying (which led to the disruption and cancellation of some classes), and a dance at the Jewish Community Center on North Prospect Avenue.

Not all student veterans, however, embraced the protests. In one incident reported by the *UWM Post,* student veterans at Milwaukee Area Technical College reportedly ripped down and burned a Viet Cong flag displayed during a rally in late 1969. What's more, some Vietnam veterans who initially protested the war soon shifted their attention to postwar issues, forming organizations to assist the growing number of returning vets. These organizations focused both on increasing employment opportunities for and improving treatment of veterans by agencies such as the VA, and on recruiting more veterans to campus.

The 1972 Federal Higher Education Amendments provided grants to universities if at least ten percent of their student body was receiving veteran educational benefits. That August, with more vets on campus, UWM celebrated Veteran Education Week, which attracted more than five hundred veterans and their families who came together to listen to speakers such as Governor Patrick Lucey, whose talk was titled "What Wisconsin Can Do for Vietnam Veterans." Participating organizations included Veterans Aiding Veterans, Interested Veterans of the Central City, and UWM's Vets' Club.

Veterans proved to be important to UWM's overall enrollment, which had grown rapidly in the 1960s and early 1970s but leveled off in the mid-1970s. However, with enhanced GI benefits drawing veterans to UWM, the number of enrolled veterans in 1974 increased to 2,603, which included 2,060 receiving benefits. In 1975, there were 2,355 veterans enrolled, with 1,831 using benefits. In 1977, however, the numbers declined to 1,675 enrolled, with 1,222 using benefits—a cause for concern among campus administrators.

The desire to recruit veterans led to efforts to better serve them, with veterans themselves becoming more involved in advocating on their own behalf. The federally funded Veterans Cost of Instruction Program (VCIP)—which required colleges to create advisory committees made up of university faculty, staff, and student veterans to help administrators meet veterans' needs—provided funding both for recruitment and on-campus services such as advising and counseling, community outreach, and special education programs. UWM's Office of Veterans Affairs, initially housed in the Admissions Office, was moved into the Office of Financial Aid in 1975, a recognition of the need to help veterans navigate the confusing financial aid and GI benefits application process. Veterans at UWM also took advantage of programs designed for students who were disadvantaged or did not meet regular admissions requirements. The Experimental Program in Higher Education (EPHE), for example, begun in 1968 out of the School of Education, enrolled thirty veteran students in 1977–1978.

But over the years, veterans at UWM continued looking for further improvements in services. The Wisconsin Veterans Union (WVU), formed in 1969, called for better benefits under federal job programs, and in 1975 held meetings to enlist veterans on campus to lobby legislators to maintain study grants for veterans. In 1978, WVU President Thomas Davis took issue with the way the university was using VCIP funds, arguing that too much money was going toward staff salaries and not enough toward the recruitment and enrollment of veterans. Indeed, veteran enrollment had declined 41 percent between 1975 and 1978. In an interview with the *UWM Post* in November 1978, Davis also criticized what was then the UWM Office of Veterans Affairs, noting complaints about its "insensitivity" and "outright hostility" toward veterans. He said the office also gave out "inadequate and

Student demonstrators march down East Kenwood Boulevard after a rally in front of Mitchell Hall to protest the United States' invasion of Cambodia ordered by President Richard M. Nixon, 1970. Photo by Alan Magayne-Roshak.

incorrect information to veterans concerning available benefits" and failed "to provide the kind of counseling veterans need." In fall 1980, veterans on campus formed a new organization, the Resisters League (RL), to counsel students against registering for the draft. In January 1981, RL members held counseling sessions with VVAW students eligible for the draft to inform them of the availability of alternative service.

As the number of African American veterans returning to Milwaukee increased, so did their presence on campus. In 1972, African American veteran students founded Interested Veterans of the Central City for Black and other minority veterans. William Sims, a Bronze Star Medal

UWM's Pershing Rifle Drill Company D-2 at the ROTC Military Ball, UWM Student Union, 1969. Photo by Alan Magayne-Roshak.

recipient, was a cofounder of the group. (Sims would go on to work for years on veterans causes in Milwaukee.) Early officers included Robert Cocroft, Jim Copeland, James Adams, Oscar Bond, and Gary Dobbs. Thomas H. Wynn Sr., a Korean War vet and UWM veteran counselor, was the faculty advisor to the group. He also helped found the National Association of Black Veterans. Wynn and Cocroft went on to serve as president and CEO, respectively, of the Center for Veterans' Issues Ltd., a Milwaukee-based organization founded in 1989 to help homeless veterans and advise agencies serving minority veterans, among other activities.

ROTC programs, which included military training and military science classes, were established on campuses across the country in the early 1900s and, in many cases, remained compulsory for male students into the 1960s. There had been ROTC programs at the UW Extension Division in Milwaukee and at the Wisconsin State College, Milwaukee prior to their merger and the creation of UWM, and in 1956, the Army ROTC program was established at UWM, its courses taught by US Army administrators who ran the program out of what was then the university's Department of Military Science. By 1968, the department was staffed by ten active-duty officers, six of whom were Vietnam veterans. That same year, the ROTC curriculum was updated, allowing students to take mainstream courses in subjects such as sociology and history to fulfill their ROTC requirements.

ROTC students at UWM could participate in the Pershing Rifle Drill Company D-2 that served as the honor guard at university functions, and

in the Society of Scabbard and Blade, an honor society made up of those in ROTC's Advance Corps. Scabbard and Blade sponsored an annual Military Ball that, according to a 1967–1968 report of the ROTC Committee, "is well attended by both military and civilian faculty, and also students." In 1967, Scabbard and Blade members sent condolence letters to Elaine Manz, the widow of 1st Lt. Terry L. Manz, a 1965 UWM graduate who died, at age twenty-five, in a helicopter crash in Vietnam. In a ceremony at Pearse Field, Elaine Manz was presented with three medals awarded posthumously to her husband: the Distinguished Flying Cross, the Bronze Star, and the Air Medal.

It is important to note that UWM ROTC students also served as a conduit to troops from the Milwaukee area who were serving in Vietnam. Although protests over the Vietnam War led to student body and faculty criticism of the ROTC program and calls for its removal in the early 1970s, the program remained an active part of campus life throughout the decade. During that contentious era, it was Col. Samuel Stroman who led UWM's ROTC program. Stroman, who had earned a master's of arts degree from Howard University and a master's of science degree from UWM, also chaired its Department of Military Science from 1970 to 1972. With the end of the Vietnam War in 1975, hostility toward ROTC declined, as did its membership. In the 1970s, the program opened membership—and participation in its Pershing drill company—to women.

In the mid-1980s, students again protested ROTC—this time for its policy of prohibiting gay and lesbian cadets from becoming officers, pointing out that state policy prohibited discrimination based on sexual orientation. Although UWM faculty voted to end ROTC, the program again hung on, remaining an official organization at UWM until the late 1980s, when federal defense budget cuts eliminated UWM's program (and its Department of Military Science) and required UWM students who wanted to participate in ROTC to take their military classes through Marquette University. Today, ROTC students split their time between Marquette and UWM, the cadets part of the Golden Eagle Battalion, which includes students from Marquette, the Milwaukee School of Engineering, Concordia University, and the University of Wisconsin-Parkside. Despite ROTC's sometimes contentious past, it continues to help many students achieve their educational goals, in part by providing eligible students with up to $80,000 over four years in financial aid.

Three decades of conflict in the Middle East, beginning in 1991, saw the deployment of more than three million US service members, many of whom would go on to complete multiple tours of duty. In response, active military and veteran students at UWM increased their involvement with faculty and staff in an effort to create an even more military-friendly campus. The veteran organizations of the 1960s and 1970s might have withered, but new organizations, created and directed by active military members and veterans, university staff, students, administrators, and faculty emerged to advocate for the needs of these students.

In 1999, for example, Veterans Upward Bound (VUB), an initiative of the US Department of Education, was established on campus. The program provided basic skills instruction and educational and career advising that helped qualified military veterans become college ready and enroll in postsecondary institutions. New policies were also put in place to accommodate the significant number of UWM students serving in US Military Reserve or National Guard units called to active duty and who, as a result, were required to temporarily postpone their educational pursuits.

▲

*Kathleen Muldowney rappelling in the Student Union during an event sponsored by ROTC, 1975.*
Photo by Alan Magayne-Roshak.

By 2007, the number of military-related and veteran students receiving benefits had surpassed eleven hundred and was steadily increasing. In response, UWM established the Military Education Benefits Office (MEBO) headed by Veterans Benefits Coordinator James Schmidt, an eight-year Army veteran who helped veterans access the wide array of military educational benefits available. Moreover, passage of the Post-9/11 Veterans Educational Assistance Act the following year further boosted veteran enrollment at state colleges and universities across Wisconsin. Today, the number of active military and veteran students receiving benefits each year at UWM regularly exceeds twelve hundred students. In 2018–2019, their average age was 30 and about 20 percent were female.

Evidence of UWM's leadership in providing additional support and protections for its military students can be found in its endorsement of President Barack Obama's 2012 executive order, Principles of Excellence for Educational Institutions Serving Service Members, Veterans, Spouses, and Other Family Members. Codified into federal law in 2021, the order calls for specific consumer

Veterans Day 2009. Attendees included veteran student Ryan James Greendeer, who voiced support for improving services to veterans, and— along with other student veterans—noted that faculty and instructors generally lacked awareness of the many military and veteran students on campus and their needs. Following Plach's presentation—and under the leadership of Vice-Chancellor and Interim Dean of Continuing Education Patricia Arredondo— she and Greendeer, along with faculty and staff representing the School of Information Studies (SOIS), MEBO, the Office of Admissions, VUB, and SAC, began to meet regularly as a subcommittee of a working group advising administrators on campus initiatives around veterans.

protections and other support for students, and essentially serves as a code of ethics for schools. Furthermore, in 2014, based on American Council on Education recommendations, UWM began awarding university-level credit for military experience as a way of helping students achieve their degrees faster. Services were also made available to veterans with disabilities through what was then UWM's Student Accessibility Center (SAC), today the Accessibility Resource Center. (Such services have been available to vets since as early as 1976 through what was then Disabled Student Services.)

In a related move, graduate student Heidi L. Plach conducted her master's research on young veterans who served in the Global War on Terrorism with a focus on their readjustment to civilian life, rates of alcohol use, and experiences with PTSD, mild traumatic brain injury, and depression. (Plach's advisor, Carol Haertlein-Sells—today professor emerita in the Department of Rehabilitation Sciences & Technology—made news when she took a leave of absence at the age of fifty-eight to enlist in the US Army, sworn in at the rank of major.) More than 90 percent of those participating in Plach's research study reported challenges such as difficulty concentrating and relating to younger classmates that affected their success in the classroom. Veterans also raised concerns about class assignments for which they were overqualified, such as requiring a medic who had drawn blood numerous times in combat to complete the same simulated lab practices and take the same exams as inexperienced students.

To share the findings of her study, Plach presented "Boots on Campus" on the eve of

The subcommittee evolved into the Veterans Advisory Council (VAC), cochaired by Arredondo and Laurie Peterson, director of the SAC. The roster of members grew to include faculty, staff, and students who were passionate about supporting student veterans at UWM. VAC member Amber Tucker helped Plach and Greendeer organize Veterans Day Recognition: Fostering a Connected Campus Community on November 11, 2010. The event, the first of its kind on campus in many years, featured a display of more than one thousand American flags, representing the number of veterans attending UWM, at Ernest Spaights Plaza. Suddenly, a near-invisible group on campus became visible and UWM was recognized the following year as a Military Friendly School by *G.I. Jobs,* a publication of Viqtory Media, a national military marketing company. At the time, only 15 percent of more than 7,000 schools and colleges were so recognized. (Viqtory Media upgraded UWM's Military Friendly designation to Silver Status for 2021–2022.) Meanwhile, Arredondo's leadership of the VAC had set the center up for continued momentum; in 2013 she passed the baton to Haertlein-Sells, another trailblazer. As a result,

MAVRC office, circa 2015.

UWM alum, veteran, and Pat Tillman Foundation Scholar Rae Anne Frey-Ho Fung. Photo courtesy Pat Tillman Foundation.

UWM continues to foster a connected community around students who are veterans or military related.

The combination of advocacy by the VAC, research into the needs of student veterans, and the active engagement of student veterans helped create a space on campus to serve veterans and those in the military who remained on active duty while at UWM. In 2012, the Military and Veteran Resource Center (MAVRC) opened in the UWM Student Union, with Michael Kirchner, a student veteran, named the center's first director. MAVRC helped bring together many important support services and offered a place for students to connect.

One of the first student veterans to benefit from the center's services was Rae Anne Frey-Ho Fung, who earned two degrees from the Department of Educational Psychology: a master's in community counseling in 2013 and a PhD in counseling psychology in 2018. At the time a single mother with two young children, Frey-Ho Fung recalled with gratitude Chancellor Mark A. Mone's attention to issues related to student veterans and diversity, Kirchner's leadership at MAVRC, the support of her degree program faculty, and the services provided by UWM's Child Care Center. "UWM wrapped its arms around me," she said. In 2013, Frey-Ho Fung became the first veteran enrolled in a Wisconsin university to be named a Pat Tillman Foundation Scholar, an honor that entitled her to scholarship aid, a national network, and professional development opportunities.

Frey-Ho Fung was the first of three UWM students to be so honored. The late Hallie Stewart-Lannan, a combat medic in the US Army, was honored with a posthumous PhD in urban education in 2020 after her death from breast cancer. Nathan Derge, whose service in the US Marine Corps gave rise to an interest in civil and human rights, received a bachelor's degree in political science and government in 2018 and went on to earn his law degree from the University of Wisconsin–Madison in 2021. From 2014 to 2017, UWM was designated a Pat Tillman Foundation University, based on programs and services for vets, such as MAVRC.

In 2012, veterans at UWM established a chapter of the national Student Veterans of America (SVA), with Kirchner as president and Lisa Coryell as vice president. David Tucek, who later served as SVA vice president, began lobbying Wisconsin lawmakers to support a bill giving student veterans and current service members priority when it came to registering for classes on campuses in the University of Wisconsin System and the Wisconsin Technical College System, a move that had been adopted elsewhere in the nation. The bill received overwhelming bipartisan support from state representatives and was signed into law in November 2013.

That same year, UWM launched a local chapter of VetSuccess on Campus (VSOC), a national program that offers veterans, service members, and their qualified dependents on-campus benefits assistance and counseling services designed to lead to the completion of a degree and entry into the labor market in viable careers. To qualify for VSOC, schools were required to enroll a minimum of eight hundred students who were receiving federal benefits for veterans. (At the time, UWM's veteran enrollment stood at 1,808.)

Meanwhile, Mone continued to value the work of the VAC, and as a way of signaling his support of the council, in 2015 designated it as one of only four such groups on campus that reported directly to him. Renamed the Veterans Advisory Council to the Chancellor (VACC), its first cochairs were Heather Hendrickson, a psychologist at the UWM's Norris Health Center; Plach, by then a clinical assistant professor of occupational therapy; and Kirchner. Plach, now a clinical associate professor, and Yolanda Medina, MAVRC director, cochair the committee today. According to its mission statement, the VACC aims "to foster a friendly and inclusive campus to promote the academic, personal, and professional goals of military and veteran students and those who engage with them through advocacy, academic resources, development of policies and practices, and educational research." Continues the statement, "As a campus resource, we will build alliances on campus and within the community to provide excellent services, ensuring military and veteran students take full advantage of their educational experience."

Both a forum for reporting on active military and veteran students' issues and a vehicle for problem-solving, advocacy, and feedback, the VACC includes among its members passionate advocates in the Office of Academic Affairs, Division of Student Affairs, and Division of Management Enrollment who have uniquely and collectively contributed to the mission of serving veterans and military students. For

▲

*US Navy veteran Ruben Burgos.*
Photo courtesy Ruben Burgos.

example, Virginia Stoffel, associate professor in the College of Health Sciences, worked with graduate students to research how Photovoice, a participatory research method that invites individuals to take photos of their everyday lives and write narratives that convey their lived experience, could help veterans document their transition from military to civilian student life, and in turn, overcome barriers and reach their educational and career goals. In a work titled "Distance," one such veteran chose a photograph of an empty highway taken from the inside of a car to illustrate her feelings, noting:

I am in my own world completely disconnected from my battle buddies who shared my experiences; the distance between us seems endless. . . . We are not only separated by physical distances but emotional as well. Even our phone conversations are brief, lacking common ground and understanding of our new experiences. People who I spent every minute of every day with for a year, who could finish my thoughts, no longer understand my life. When I returned to the States, we demobilized at Fort McCoy for four to five days and were scattered to the wind, left to our own devices to navigate the civilian world. . . . This is just the nature of the military; people come together from all over the country for a common purpose and return once they are finished. Campuses need to create student veteran's organizations to get student veterans connected with others who feel our losses. Don't judge, connect veterans with other veterans on campus.

Many of the achievements of the VACC and MAVRC and much of the success of student veterans over the past fifteen years can be traced back to Schmidt, a VACC member who has worked tirelessly to ensure that more than fifteen

◀

*Ruben Burgos, today a UWM senior lecturer, with his wife, Maria Burgos, and Pounce the Panther.*
Photo courtesy Ruben Burgos.

a result, when the Gulf crisis broke out in August 1990, he was sent to Saudi Arabia to coordinate the formation of a coalition of thirty-seven disparate nations—a truly historic event promoting international cooperation for the common good. UWM honored Schwartz in spring 1991 with UWM's first Alumni Association Special Achievement Award, now known as the UWM Alumni Association Lifetime Achievement Award.

Ruben Burgos was recruited into the US Navy in 1986 after earning a bachelor's degree in political science from UWM. One of very few (and at times, only) officers of color, he served on active duty until 1988 and in the Naval Reserves from 1988 to 1996, working as a lieutenant in intelligence. After leaving active duty, Burgos came home to work for the Milwaukee Police Department; upon retirement, he earned a master's degree in adult education from Springfield College in Springfield, Massachusetts, before returning to UWM where today he is a senior lecturer in the Department of Criminal Justice and Criminology.

James "Groovy" Cocroft served as an operations specialist in the US Navy from 1987 to 2007. With the support of family and coworkers, who encouraged him to start the next chapter of his life, he transitioned to being a student at UWM.

thousand student veterans and their dependents have received the benefits they earned and, as a result, were able to focus on their goals of obtaining a degree at UWM. Schmidt also has been instrumental in retaining student veterans and active members of the military at UWM and connecting them to UWM researchers, amplifying their voices and preserving their legacies.

Countless other UWM graduates and staff members who served in the military also contributed to the campus and beyond, including a number of UWM graduates from the 1950s who became important in the military long after they were students. Paul R. Schwartz, for example, a ROTC student who earned a bachelor's of science degree in biology in 1959, entered the army and rose to the rank of major general and served as US General Norman Schwartzkopf Jr.'s special assistant for coalition warfare in Operation Desert Storm. Schwartz served for thirty-two years in the US Army, helping to modernize the Saudi Arabian National Guard and a multinational hospital in Riyadh from 1985 to 1988. As

*James "Groovy" Cocroft, US Navy veteran, returns from Iraq, 2003.*
Photo courtesy James Cocroft.

▶

Cocroft's military experience—which included experience with data link systems, communication equipment, and electronic charting systems—influenced his decision to pursue a degree in information science and technology at SOIS. A few years after graduation, he became assistant director of MAVRC, a position he holds today. Cocroft said he relies on his personal experience to not only help students who are veterans or members of the military navigate the university system, but also support their academic and emotional well-being. Notes Cocroft, "I want them to have the best experience here and for them to be successful in their studies and beyond."

One of UWM's most notable women veterans is Miriam Ben-Shalom, who earned her undergraduate and graduate degrees in creative writing from UWM before enlisting in the US Army in 1974. Open about her sexual orientation, Ben-Shalom—who was a lesbian—was discharged after serving two years of a three-year tour of duty. She appealed her discharge and, following a long court battle, was reinstated by a federal judge in 1980. The Army delayed compliance until 1987 (and only after being threatened with large fines), when Ben-Shalom became the first LGBTQ+ service member reinstated in the US military after having been discharged. Prohibited from reenlistment, Ben-Shalom nevertheless played an integral role in repealing Don't Ask, Don't Tell, the US policy in effect from 1994 to 2011 that prevented gay, lesbian, and bisexual individuals from openly serving in the military.

Yolanda Medina served in the US Marine Corps from 1980 to 1985, training as one of the Corps' first female environmental systems technicians and working on the AV8-A and AV8-B Harrier attack aircraft. After completing her military service, Medina joined the American GI Forum (a Latinx veterans advocacy organization) and helped create the Wisconsin Latino Veterans Memorial Foundation to document the service of Wisconsin's Latinx veterans. Medina serves as a member of the board of directors of both the Latino Veterans Legacy of Valor and Forward Latino, where she is its advisor on Latino veterans' issues. In 2018, she became the director of MAVRC.

In 2017, women veterans in Portland, Oregon, launched the "I Am Not Invisible" campaign to draw attention to the problems female service members and veterans faced when attempting to access health care and other benefits. The Center for Women Veterans at the US Department of Veterans Affairs subsequently created a national pictorial and oral history campaign to bring attention to the diverse community of women who wore the uniform of the US military. The Wisconsin display, housed at the Wisconsin Veterans Museum in Madison, honors Medina and two other women with ties to UWM: Kimberly Stuart, UWM alum and a US Air Force veteran and Air Force National Guard member; and Tiffany Koehler, a current UWM student and a US Army veteran.

Adam Wickersham was a UWM student double majoring in economics and international studies and an active service member on September 11, 2001. Today the director of master's degree programs in the Sheldon B. Lubar School of Business and a member of VACC, Wickersham recounted some of what he experienced in the wake of that fateful day, noting that "three days later, I was in New York City sifting through rubble.

*Yolanda Medina and her husband, Joe Medina, at US Marine Corps Boot Camp, 1981.* Photo courtesy Yolanda Medina.

*Jayne Holland, Cesar Pabon, and Yolanda Medina (left to right) at the Vets Ball, 2018.* Photo by Elora Hennessey.

One year later, I was at Bagram Air Base. Two years after that, I was on an Iraqi farm outside Tikrit inside a spider hole staring at Saddam Hussein." Wickersham would serve three tours of duty, endure four surgeries, and attend forty-three military funerals before he graduated from UWM. According to Wickersham, the fall of Afghanistan to the Taliban when US troops pulled out of the country in 2021 was "proof of the great things"— such as a reduction in the rates of infant mortality and illiteracy—"that our soldiers, airmen, marines, and coasties [had been] able to accomplish." Wickersham, who went on to earn an MBA in 2013, also praised UWM for its unsurpassed veteran services.

Plach sees Wickersham as an incredible role model. "Adam exemplifies the kind of resilience and dedication displayed by so many military-related students and faculty," she said. "He demonstrates the sacrifice and contributions they have made not only to our country, but also to our campus and the local community."

Today, UWM enrolls the most veterans of any university in Wisconsin and is considered one of the top destinations for military and veteran students in the Midwest. Campus leaders have prioritized responding to the needs of veterans and supported UWM's extensive programs for students who are veterans or members of the military. Moreover, many of UWM's military and veteran services are

*Three generations of veterans (left to right) Sawyer Wickersham, who served in Iraq, Afghanistan, and Syria; Sawyer's grandfather, Bernie Wickersham, who served in Vietnam; and Sawyer's father, who served in Iraq and Afghanistan.* Photo courtesy Adam Wickersham.

directed by veterans who best understand the needs of their peers on campus. The impact of investing in building the social and intellectual capital of UWM's military and veteran students continues to unfold as students, alumni, faculty, and staff make significant contributions ranging from on-campus initiatives to programs in Milwaukee and beyond that serve this unique population.

# AFTERWORD

It is my hope that as you completed your reading of *Telling Our Stories* it was through a lens of ongoing opportunity, recognizing the ways in which this important book serves as a hallmark of how we best document history. In its truest form, history should be an accurate and inclusive representation of what has occurred when one looks back over one's shoulder. It is often told by those with a love of an era and a willingness to cement its stories for generations yet to come.

Notably, *Telling Our Stories* does just that, highlighting the experiences of cohorts of individuals whose lives have been historically unrepresented—their voices all too often supplanted by others not reflective of an authentic and culturally comprehensive approach. This specially commissioned volume, featuring the work of an inclusive array of contributing authors, outlines the diverse contributions and lived realities that went into building the University of Wisconsin-Milwaukee (UWM), the most diverse institution in the University of Wisconsin System. In so doing, it paints a picture of a university where dreams were—and continue to be—visualized, and where futures are filled with possibility.

The year was 1971 when I first traversed the doors of this institution. As a wide-eyed freshman, the last thing on my mind was how my dreams and future would be shaped by any of the individuals recognized in these chapters. If I had only known! The civil rights movement was still at its peak and UWM was in the early stages of diversifying its faculty and student body. Additionally, dedicated men and women were taking bold steps to enrich the student experience, such as establishing programs in new, exciting academic disciplines and opening multicultural student centers as ways to provide an inclusive, welcoming, and supportive environment where all students, regardless of their backgrounds, could thrive and succeed.

*Telling Our Stories* grew out of the belief that accounts of UWM's institutional history needed to document these kinds of inclusive efforts and that failing to reflect on the accomplishments of the key players involved was not an option. As a result, this book serves as an acknowledgment that those contributors deserve the same level of respect paid others in the past. It is notable as well that those whose faces and names are spotlighted—along with those not recognized in print—did their work without the expectation of recognition, but rather to provide a roadmap for their colleagues and successors. That kind of dedication continues to inspire, serving to motivate a new generation working to find ways to teach and learn in a welcoming, bias-free environment.

There is an important lesson to be learned from the way in which this book was conceived and created. If history is, in fact, a compilation of memories and experiences to be treasured and passed down through generations, any work chronicling a historical journey must be told in the voices of its participants. Moreover, the opportunity to hear from a wide, rich mosaic of voices not only enriches such stories, but also contributes to the authenticity and transparency of the intent driving the work. Indeed, there is no better way to shape these stories than through the eyes of each cohort that gave of themselves and collaborated with others—in this case, to ensure the success of UWM.

It should be noted that this book is not intended to relegate the history of diversity at UWM to a single collection of separate stories—often a response to what was not included in a first "go-round"—but rather to take the opportunity to highlight a deliberate, strategic, and intentional part of our institutional history, one that celebrates much of what has made UWM the world-class bastion of higher education that it is today. Consider, for example, that stories such as those highlighted here document work, over the years, from which all students have benefitted.

Sustained change always starts at the top. In this case, the change agent was Chancellor Mark A. Mone. Special thanks to you, Chancellor Mone, for never blinking an eye when I approached you about the need for an inclusive rendition of our institutional history. You never asked why it was needed, simply noting that it was long overdue and that together we would make it happen. Because of your support and that of other administrative team members, this history has come to fruition and can sit proudly with its peers in the archives, permanently linked to this institution. My thanks to Vice-Chancellor and Professor Chia Youyee Vang and Associate Professor David J. Pate Jr., the scholars responsible for taking an idea and seeing it to fruition, and who continue to work tirelessly every day to ensure that the diverse voices of current and future faculty, staff, and students will never be excluded from the history of this institution. That same heartfelt thank-you is extended to each and every contributing author. Your work will forever be viewed as the heart and soul of *Telling Our Stories*.

As a four-time UWM alumna with more than twenty years of experience as one of its administrators, I see this book—as I hope you do as well—as an authentic account of a critically important part of our institution's history recounted in the voices of its architects. In stories that speak to

accomplishments achieved and challenges ahead, they remind us of the richness of UWM's journey to date and the promise of its future.

Joan M. Prince, PhD
Vice-Chancellor Emerita
University of Wisconsin-Milwaukee
June 2022

# ACKNOWLEDGMENTS

## CHAPTER 1:
### Michael Wilson and Margaret Noodin

We would like to acknowledge and thank the ancestors who stewarded this space before us and were teaching and helping others to find their places in the web of life long before universities had buildings. Thanks as well to those who contributed to our efforts: Diane Amour, Kim Blaeser, Siobhan Marks, Colleen Boatman Katchenago, Mike Connors, Janice Rice, Susan Wade, Nathon Breu, Sommer Drake, Sue Chicks-Wojciechowski, and Angela Mesic. And for her patient help with images and documents, as well as her long dedication to American Indian students on the UWM campus, we thank Celeste Clark.

## CHAPTER 2:
### David J. Pate Jr., H. Victoria Pryor, and Derrick Vaughn Langston

We are enormously grateful to these individuals who shared their time and stories with us on their lived experiences at UWM: Reuben Harpole; Akbar Ally, PhD; Kathy Berry; Brenda Cullin; Gary Williams, PhD; Joan Prince, PhD; Kelby Spann; Portia Cobb; Ferne Yangyeitie Caulker-Bronson; Susan Fields; Diana Edwards; Milton Coleman; Frederick Gordon; Daniel Burrell; Mohammed Aman, PhD; April Holland; Doris Johnson (Brown), PhD; James Peoples, PhD; Sandra Million-Underwood, PhD; Leonard White; John Pinkston; Teresa Buchanan; Patrick Bellegarde-Smith, PhD; Anika Wilson, PhD; Kent Wilburn; Elizabeth Drame, PhD; Wilkistar Otieno, PhD; Anita Sparks; and Frank Wilson, PhD. We are thankful to you for participating with us in this academic endeavor to document our history of contributions to UWM.

## CHAPTER 3:
### Joseph A. Rodríguez and William Vélez

The authors are grateful to Chancellor Carlos E. Santiago for providing documents and other information regarding his years at UWM. Joseph A. Rodríguez also thanks Susan Hunter for sharing her research on the history of the Spanish Speaking Outreach Institute.

## CHAPTER 4:
### Chia Youyee Vang, Linda Huang, and Adrian Chan

Because limited archival materials exist on the experiences of people of Asian descent at UWM for us to consult, we thank the many people who responded to our questions electronically, by phone, or through oral interviews: Swarnjit Arora, Yea-Fen Chen, Kyoung Ae Cho, Patti Cobb, Emraida Kiram, Alice Kuramoto, Susie Lamborn, Gwat-Yong Lie, Ron Podeschi, Channy Rasavong, Pradeep Rohatgi, Kumkum Sangari, Shinji Takahashi, Hanh Trinh, Keh Tsao, Dao Vang, Ger Vang, Devarajan Venugopalan, and Ge Xiong. We also benefitted greatly from the fact that Adrian and Linda had been intimately involved in diversity/multicultural efforts over the last four decades and had first-hand knowledge to share. Finally, we are especially indebted to Dev Venugopalan for helping to verify information.

## CHAPTER 5:
### Gwynne Kennedy and Merry Wiesner-Hanks

We are very grateful to the following, who agreed to be interviewed for this chapter: Pamela Boulton, Krista Grensavitch, Jamakaya, Connie Jo, Justice

Johnson, Cheryl Kader, Pat Kissinger, Kathy Miller-Dillon, Kim Romenesko, Erika Sander, Peggy Silvestri, and Lori Vance. And for further help with research, thanks to Margo Anderson, Shane Dunlap, Nadya Fouad, Laurie Glass, Ann Hanlon, Sally Lundeen, Alan Magayne-Roshak, Cathy Seasholes, Caterina Sukup, and the entire staff of the Archives Department of the UWM Libraries.

## CHAPTER 6:
### Michael Doylen and Jennifer (Jen) Murray

We wish to thank Cary Costello, Thomas Dake, and Jeffrey Merrick, who agreed to be interviewed for this chapter. Thanks, also, to the staff of the Archives Department of the UWM Libraries, who provided access to the primary sources needed to tell this story, and the UWM Lesbian, Gay, Bisexual, Transgender, Queer Plus Resource Center.

## CHAPTER 7:
### Jonathan Broskowski, Christi Craig, and Roger O. Smith

UWM has a long history of recognizing and supporting students, faculty, and staff with disabilities and leading the field of accessibility in higher education. This was made possible due to the energy and activism of the UWM community, which pushed the university to provide better physical access on campus and equal learning opportunities for persons with disabilities long before required by federal law. These early efforts provided a pathway for how disability is viewed at UWM today and established a solid framework and a creative vision for accessibility in the twenty-first century. We wish to thank all those who laid the groundwork for the comprehensive disability services and proactive projects at UWM that provide for current and future generations of UWM students, faculty, staff, and visitors.

## CHAPTER 8:
### Tracy Buss and Devarajan Venugopalan

We greatly appreciate the contributions of current and former students, faculty, and staff to our chapter on campus internationalization at UWM. Interviews with Swarnjit Arora, Ewa Barczyk, Johannes Britz, Julie Kline, Peter Lee, Donald Pienkos, Mark Tessler, Violeta Ramirez, Yenbo Wu,

and David Yu helped provide historical information on campus internationalization that we could not have found in the Archives Department of the UWM Libraries. Additionally, we gathered valuable insights using two questionnaires, with respondents including—but not limited to—Mohsen Bahmani-Oskooee, Anne Dressel, Neel Kamal Chapagain, Jorge Hernández, Magdalena Irigaray, Kemal Pelit, and Sara Tully. Center for International Education colleagues Sharon Gosz, Jennifer Gruenewald, and Doug Savage also reviewed and contributed to this chapter.

## CHAPTER 9:
### Heidi L. Plach, Yolanda Medina, Joseph A. Rodríguez, and Virginia Stoffel

Words alone cannot express the gratitude we have for all those contributing to this chapter. First, we'd like to acknowledge the former student veterans, including UWM's Vets' Club members, who graciously shared not only memories of their days at UWM but also valuable archival material and photos. Second, we'd like to thank the faculty and staff veterans who also allowed us to capture their experiences in service of our country and our university. Our deepest thanks as well go to our colleagues on the Veterans Advisory Council to the Chancellor (VACC), and those working in the Military and Veterans Resource Center (MAVRC) and Military Education Benefits Office (MEBO), who were willing to share with us their considerable institutional knowledge even as they continue to trailblaze innovative ways to support military-related and veteran students. A special thanks to Elora Hennessey, who went out of her way to retrieve and take many of the photos that appear in the chapter. Last, but not least, we greatly appreciate all those who made themselves available for interviews: Guy Porth, Douglas "Radar" Lueck, Pat Eisenhart, Ned Redding, Lloyd Steiner, Rollie Pieper, Phil Yakish, Ted DiStefano, Carol Haertlein-Sells, Rae Anne Ho Fung, Ruben Burgos, James "Groovy" Crocroft, and Adam Wickersham.

# ABOUT THE CONTRIBUTORS

**Jonathan Broskowski, MS,** has been with the Accessibility Resource Center at UWM since 1999 and has served as the center's Interim Director since 2019. During his time at UWM—and beyond his focus on access/inclusion/accommodation—Broskowski has served as chair, cochair, secretary, and team member of several university committees that foster and nurture efforts to promote student success. Applying principles of vocational rehabilitation to his work, Broskowski has not only aided students in making the most of their educational experiences but also helped them prepare to enter the workforce.

**Tracy Buss, DBA,** joined the UWM Center for International Education (CIE) in 2005, and today serves as its Associate Director for International Partnerships and Market Development. Buss previously worked as the center's Assistant Director of Academic and Research Programs when CIE was home to the Global Studies and International Studies programs and UWM's Global Studies Fellows. Buss has conducted research on decision making and information behavior in the college search process.

**Adrian Chan, PhD,** is Professor Emeritus of Educational Psychology who specialized in multicultural/counseling psychology. Chan was one of the first Asian American diversity leaders at UWM. As an Assistant Vice-Chancellor in the Office of Multicultural Affairs, he was responsible for drafting Milwaukee Initiative II, a response to the UW System's Design for Diversity. He later served as Director of the UW System's Institute on Race and Ethnicity.

**Christi Craig, BA,** is the Assistive Technology Coordinator in UWM's Accessibility Resource Center. She began her career at UWM as an intern with the Deaf and Hard of Hearing Program in spring 1998 and was hired as a Staff Interpreter that fall. Craig is coauthor (with Margaret Noodin) of "Deaf-centric and Sovereign: Translation as a Tool for Changing Audism and English Dominance," published by *Altre Modernità /Otras modernidades/ Autres modernités/Other modernities* in 2019.

**Michael Doylen, PhD,** (he/him) is Associate Vice-Provost and Director of the UWM Libraries. Doylen has spent his entire professional career in academic libraries, mainly at UWM. He served as the Head of Archives from 2003 to 2016; as Assistant Director of Archives, Special Collections, and the Music Library from 2012 to 2019; and as Interim Associate Vice-Provost and Director of Libraries from 2016 to 2019.

**Linda Huang, MS,** Academic Staff Emerita, joined the Multicultural/Disadvantaged Coordinators Office in the late 1980s, rising to the rank of Administrative Program Manager III. Huang's responsibilities throughout her professional career at UWM focused mostly on providing support services to multicultural students and assisting in the coordination of campus-wide diversity efforts.

**Gwynne Kennedy, PhD,** is Associate Professor Emerita of English and Women's & Gender Studies. Her research and teaching interests include early modern women writers and theories and politics of emotions. Kennedy was active in Women's & Gender Studies for more than thirty years, serving as its director from 2006 to 2013 and its chair from 2018 to 2019.

**Derrick Vaughn Langston, MA,** Multicultural Student Success Coordinator with the Black Student Cultural Center, is pursuing a doctoral degree examining intercultural communication with a specific interest in how Black students create and maintain social support systems at predominately white institutions.

**Yolanda Medina, MEd,** is director of the Military and Veterans Resource Center. She served in the US Marine Corps from 1980 to 1985 and is active in efforts to support Latinx veterans.

**Jennifer (Jen) Murray, MPH,** (they, them, theirs and she, her, hers) has been connected to UWM since 2004, focusing on work with marginalized and minoritized populations. They served as the Interim Director of Gender and Sexuality Advocacy, working with both the LGBTQ+ Resource Center and the Women's Resource Center. Murray is invested in dialogue and healing transformation through self-awareness and remains committed to dismantling systems of power and privilege that recreate patterns of injustice using a heart-centered approach.

**Margaret Noodin, PhD,** is Professor of English, Director of UWM's Electa Quinney Institute for American Indian Education, and Associate Dean, Humanities, in the College of Letters & Science. Noodin's research and teaching interests include Indigenous and American Indian literature and culture, language revitalization, language pedagogy and curriculum, Anishinaabemowin poetry and stories, and global Indigenous intellectual traditions.

**David J. Pate Jr., PhD,** is Associate Professor and Chair of the Department of Social Work in the Helen Bader School of Social Welfare, and an Affiliated Associate Professor at the Institute for Research on Poverty at the University of Wisconsin–Madison. Pate's research and teaching involves examining the life course events of Black lives, and specifically those of Black men, and the social welfare policy affecting their lives. He is a member of Kappa Alpha Psi fraternity, Alpha Beta Chapter.

**Heidi L. Plach, MS, OTR/L,** is Clinical Associate Professor and Academic Fieldwork Coordinator in the Occupational Therapy program. Plach's clinical practice background is in community mental health, and for over two decades she has volunteered with the National Alliance on Mental Illness, facilitating family support groups and training frontline employees, such as first responders, in crisis intervention. Plach has published research on the experiences of young veterans returning to civilian life after serving in the Global War on Terrorism and has been instrumental in advancing grassroots initiatives related to improving the climate on campus for students who are veterans or active military members. Since 2015, Plach has served as cochair of UWM's Veterans Advisory Council to the Chancellor.

**H. Victoria Pryor, MS,** is the Student Services Program Manager at the Black Student Cultural Center. She began her UWM career in community and governmental relations and has worked with all constituencies during her more than thirty years at the university. Pryor is a lifetime member of Alpha Kappa Alpha sorority, Upsilon Mu Omega Chapter.

**Joseph A. Rodríguez, PhD,** is Professor of History and Urban Studies specializing in and teaching classes on US, Latino, Asian American, urban, and transportation history. Rodríguez's books include *City against Suburb: The Culture Wars in an American Metropolis* (Prager, 1999), *Bootstrap New Urbanism: Race and Redevelopment in Milwaukee* (Lexington, 2014), and *Latinos in Milwaukee* (coauthored with Walter Sava) (Arcadia, 2000).

**Roger O. Smith, PhD, OT, FAOTA,** is Professor of Occupational Therapy, Sciences, and Technology who joined the UWM faculty in 1994. Since then, he has led more than thirty-five training, demonstration, and research projects pertaining to disability sciences with a focus on technology interventions and accessibility. Globally recognized in his field, Smith is a past president of the Rehabilitation Engineering and Assistive Technology Society of North America (RESNA) and a RESNA Fellow. He has served on the National Advisory Board on Medical Rehabilitation Research at the National Institutes of Health, and on the boards of the National Science Foundation and the National Institute on

Disability, Independent Living, and Rehabilitation Research. He has also consulted with the World Health Organization on its global assistive technology initiative.

**Virginia Stoffel, PhD,** is Associate Professor of Occupational Therapy, and has been preparing future occupational therapists at UWM since 1982. Her research interests include the effect on recovery of mental health and substance use disorders, and the lived experiences of veterans transitioning from military to civilian student life. Stoffel serves on the Veterans Advisory Council to the Chancellor, offering her perspective as a faculty member and a military family member (mother of a Navy submariner, daughter of a Navy World War II pilot). Stoffel is coauthor of a mental health occupational therapy text that is used in graduate programs worldwide, is past president of the American Occupational Therapy Association (AOTA), and currently represents the AOTA to the World Federation of Occupational Therapists.

**Chia Youyee Vang, PhD,** is Vice-Chancellor for Diversity, Equity, and Inclusion and Professor of History. She served as Associate Vice-Chancellor in the Division of Global Inclusion and Engagement from 2017 to 2021. Vang has authored four books, edited two scholarly volumes, and written more than two dozen articles/reports on the impact of global displacement on refugees from the Vietnam War era.

**William Vélez, PhD,** is Professor Emeritus of Sociology. His scholarship is broadly focused on educational and housing issues with specialized research interests in Latino urban populations. Vélez has published articles in *Sociology of Education, Social Science Research, Journal of Latinos and Education,* and *Urban Affairs Review.*

**Devarajan Venugopalan, PhD,** is Associate Vice-Chancellor for Academic Affairs and Associate Professor of Materials Science & Engineering. His research interests include materials processing and manufacturing. Venugopalan served as chair of the Department of Materials Science & Engineering from 1996 to 1998 and as Associate Dean in the College of Engineering & Applied Science from 1998 to 2004.

**Merry Wiesner-Hanks, PhD,** is Distinguished Professor Emerita of History and Women's & Gender Studies and served twice as the director of Women's & Gender Studies and three times as chair of the Department of History. She is the author or editor of more than thirty books that have appeared in ten European and Asian languages, including a number on women's and gender history.

**Michael Wilson, PhD,** is Associate Professor of English and Director of American Indian Studies. His research and teaching interests include Indigenous literatures of North America and postcolonial theory.